Boss
is a four
letter word!

Boss

is a four letter word!

How to reduce STRESS, increase PRODUCTIVITY and improve EMPLOYEE RELATIONS, plus 32 steps to leadership for results.

Brian Spikes

General Publishing Co. Limited
Don Mills, Ontario

Published 1977 by
General Publishing Co. Limited
Don Mills, Ontario

Fourth Printing 1982

Canadian Cataloguing in Publication Data

Spikes, Brian.
  Boss is a four letter word!

Bibliography: p.
ISBN 0-7736-1028-6

1. Management.   2. Leadership.   3. Supervisors.
I. Title.

1st printing
HD31.S65   658.4   C77-001245-0

Printed and bound in Canada

CONTENTS

About the Author

Brian Spikes
Canadian Author, Consultant and Instructor

Brian Spikes has conducted successful seminars in Human Resources Management for more than ten thousand supervisors and managers across Canada during the last eight years. He has spoken to the employees of major business and industrial corporations, associations, hospitals, universities, colleges, and federal, provincial and municipal agencies. He has been interviewed on numerous television and radio programs in Canada and overseas and he is in frequent demand to conduct presentations on future shock, time management, human relations, the human energy crisis, managing for results and leadership in management.

Foreword

This book owes its existence to requests and ideas from many participants in many seminars which I have conducted in Canada during the past six years as a management instructor and consultant.

I have learned that few managers can find the time to do much heavy reading, but that they are grateful for concise and readable material that pulls together some strands of what is already known in the vast field of management and leadership. This book tries to meet their need, but it will also interest those who work for a Boss or a Leader, or both.

The informed reader will find nothing particularly new in these pages, but he will find a new perspective. Hundreds of excellent books have been written on management, and wherever possible I have tried to document the main sources of my inspiration.

If just a few readers are encouraged to learn more about the vital subject of leadership in management, I shall be well pleased.

Brian Spikes

Preface

The continuing demand for this book reflects a growing awareness and concern over the fact that something is desperately wrong in the way most people are managed in the world of work. More and more managers are beginning to learn that high productivity does not come from increasing wages and salaries, it comes from improving the quality of leadership at all levels of an organization.

The recent revelation that Japanese workers are far more productive than North American workers is not due to a difference in "culture", it is due to a difference in management. This has been clearly established by studies which show that Japanese-managed companies in the U.S. are outperforming American companies in the same industries. These studies demonstrate that new approaches, new methods, and new attitudes toward employees can very significantly improve productivity and the quality of work.

This book attempts to give perspective and practical expression to many of these new approaches to leadership in the world of work.

Once again, I should like to express my appreciation for the support and encouragement I have received from many organizations and individuals across Canada and overseas.

Brian Spikes
Toronto 1981

A LEADER

A Leader is best
When people barely know that he exists,
Not so good when people obey and acclaim him
Worst when they despise him
'Fail to honour
They fail to honour you';
But a good leader, who talks little,
When his word is done, his objective reached,
They will all say, "We did this ourselves".

Lao-Tzu

This book is dedicated to my colleagues and fellow workers in the world of work who are committed to improving the quality of working life for all Canadians.

Brian Spikes
Toronto 1981

Chapter 1

"Baas"

IN THE BEGINNING WAS THE WORD

The term "BOSS" comes from the Dutch word BAAS
Which means MASTER.

★ ★ ★

The term MASTER implies the existence
of SERVANTS

★ ★ ★

Have you hired any "SERVANTS" lately?

★ ★ ★

If you say "NO" you may be a Leader.
If you say "YES" — you *are* a Boss.

★ ★ ★

There are "Bosses" from top to bottom
in almost every organization.
Everyone has a good name for them. They whisper it.

11

Why does Canada have the worst strike record in the world? Why is productivity in Canada declining? Why is there endless conflict between management and labor? Why do thousands of Canadians find work boring?

According to the Economic Council, Canada's record of productivity is the lowest in the Western World, and it is not going to improve over the next decade. Canada's year-to-year growth is expected to be around 2%. The Economic Council has stated that low productivity has put Canada in a position that threatens its standard of living, and its ability to function as a nation.

From coast-to-coast, eminent speakers spell out the fate that awaits us unless we achieve some kind of economic salvation. Mind you, they don't tell us *how* we can do it, they just tell us we *must* do it. And so we are confronted with the spectacle of everyone urging everyone else to work together in harmony. Somehow, Business, Government, and Labor are supposed to get together in a blaze of goodwill and save the economy at the eleventh hour. Fat chance.

Business, Government, and Labor do seem to agree on at least one point: if things were somehow different, the combined efforts of employees across the land would significantly improve national productivity.

So what's the problem? What is holding employees back? No doubt there are many causes for the problems facing our economy but one of the most important is rarely discussed.

I believe that Canada has too many Bosses and too few Leaders. I believe that Bosses are responsible for more than half of the problems that afflict many of our biggest factories, government departments, and business institutions. In my experience as a management consultant I have seen dramatic evidence of the way Bosses turn people off, and reduce productivity, and how Leaders turn people on, and increase productivity.

The reason for this is very clear: Bosses drive, Leaders lead. Bosses drive because they don't know how to lead. They drive their people up the wall. Bosses believe that employees should work hard and obey orders. They worry too much about getting people to do things right, instead of getting people to do the right things. Bosses like "little" people who obey orders, never ask questions, and wait to be told what to do and how to do it.

Leaders, on the other hand, help their employees to grow on the job, develop their potential, accept responsibility, and use initiative. Leaders know that their most important responsibility as a manager or supervisor is to develop employees to the standard of performance required to do a job well, and to do it willingly.

Unfortunately, Bosses greatly outnumber Leaders and their total effect on the national economy can only be guessed. But when individual examples of Bosses and Leaders are compared in terms of results, the implications are staggering.

Billions of dollars have been spent in search of techniques and mechanical devices to improve performance and productivity, and the search goes on for a new machine that will do the job faster and cheaper. In most cases, however, management has overlooked our greatest national resource: the natural desire of the vast majority of Canadians to be engaged in doing something challenging and worthwhile. Somehow management has lost sight of those fundamental forces that can raise people above their limitations and lead them on to great achievements. When disaster strikes ordinary people do extraordinary things. Why is it that management is seldom able to release the potential of its employees?

For better or worse we have learned to unleash the potential of the atom. Is it too much to expect that management should learn how to unleash the potential of people in the world-of-work? It can be done, and it is being done, in organizations where Leaders outnumber Bosses.

The inability of management to harness the full potential of human energy in the world-of-work is one of the major reasons for continuing crises in labor relations. Human beings have become experts in applying all kinds of non-human energy for a multitude of purposes. But now, in the 1970's, we are face-to-face with the incredible fact that most managers do not know how to apply human energy effectively. There is much ado about the fuel energy crisis; how often do you hear about the human energy crisis? Most people at work are operating far below their true capacity.

To a large extent management is responsible for this situation, this human energy crisis in the world-of-work, because, in most cases, management has failed to apply leadership know-how in harnessing human energy.

The key to unleashing human energy at work lies in helping Bosses to become Leaders by showing them that Leaders get better results. Bosses operate under negative assumptions about workers that have dominated the world-of-work for centuries. Bosses are still in the Stone Age when it comes to understanding and applying the unlimited potential of Human Resources.

This is what this book attempts to do. It is about the way people manage or are managed in the world-of-work, and that includes just about everybody. Whether you like it or not, you work to live . . . and you live to work. Why? Because work is any activity that has value to others. So, whether you are an engineer, postman, salesman, clerk, nurse, or whatever, this book will interest you because it compares the influence of Bosses and Leaders on the performance and productivity of employees in any kind of work situation.

If you are a manager or supervisor you are responsible for getting things done through other people. Reading this book will help you to decide whether you are a Boss or a Leader. If you discover that you are a BOSS, don't despair. You can learn to be a Leader, because Leaders are not born, they are made. If you attempt sincerely to apply the guidelines outlined in this book your employees will improve their performance and productivity, and almost certainly, they will be much easier to get along with.

Management can be defined as "organization for survival", and economic survival is a critical issue for everyone in the 1970's. The way in which managers and supervisors get things done through other people has a profound influence on performance and productivity at every level of every kind of organization. It has far reaching effects on the health and welfare of 10 million employees across the land, and

15

indirectly, it influences the quality of democratic government.

History has taught us that organizations and nations which survive are those which inspire and challenge their members to give of their uttermost. This requires leadership of the highest order.

Unless Bosses change and become Leaders, our economy will collapse into social and economic chaos.

BARE FACTS ABOUT THE NAKED TRUTH

According to statistics published by Britain's Department of Employment Canada has the worst strike record among industrialized countries. In 1975, Canada lost more than five times as many man days for every 1000 employed as Britain. Canada lost 2840 days for every 1000 employed, 1200 more than Italy (the second worst record) and 1450 more than third-place Australia.

DO YOU WORK FOR A BOSS ... OR FOR A LEADER?
TRY THIS QUIZ

YES   NO

1) Do you feel that in your work you are using your full ability?
2) Do you feel that your job is really important?
3) Are you able to decide how you do your work?
4) Do you get recognition for a job well done?

5) Do you know what results you are expected to achieve?
6) Do you get regular and constructive feed-back on how you are doing?
7) Do you find your work interesting most of the time?
8) When your work is completed do you feel you have achieved something worthwhile?
9) Do you feel that your supervisor is interested in you as a person?
10) If your relatives or friends ask you about your work, do you like to talk about it?

If you answer NO to most of these questions you are working for a Boss.

If you answer YES to most of the questions, you are working for a Leader.

What difference does it make? It could make a big difference to you, in terms of job satisfaction and earnings, family and social relationships, to your employer, and finally, to the whole economy.

ARE YOU A BOSS OR A LEADER?
TRY THIS QUIZ

                                              YES   NO

1) Can you state clearly and precisely why you are on the payroll?
2) Can you state clearly and precisely the nature of the business you are in?
3) Can you state clearly and precisely the nature of your most important responsibility?
4) Do you know how your employees could give themselves a 10% increase in their

salary without your knowing anything about it?

5) Can you state clearly and precisely how you know when you have done a good job?

6) Do you know why you should listen nine times more than you talk?

7) Do you know why you should ask three times as many questions as you give answers?

8) Can you state clearly and precisely who your customers are, both internally and externally?

9) Can you state clearly and precisely what your customers are paying you for?

10) Do you deliberately and frequently get your people involved in making decisions about the way they work, and the results they obtain?

If you find it difficult to answer any of these questions the chances are high that you are a Boss. Remember this, a Boss may be very *efficient* but he may also be very *ineffective*. If you worry more about doing things *right*, than doing the *right things*, you are definitely a Boss. If you are willing to follow a prescription for change you may be able to increase the productivity of your people very dramatically. Any prescription has to be carefully made up in the right amount. Home remedies brewed up by chance are worse than useless. Like any powerful drug, change can keep you healthy when taken in the right amounts, but an overdose can be dangerous.

WHO GETS THE BEST RESULTS . . . BOSSES OR LEADERS?
CHECK YOUR OWN EXPERIENCE

PUT A CHECK MARK AGAINST THE DESCRIPTION THAT MOST NEARLY DESCRIBES THE MOST PRODUCTIVE GROUP, OR DEPARTMENT, YOU HAVE EVER KNOWN.

FIRST LIST

1) Information flowed through established channels. Most communication was between superiors and subordinates.

2) People were told what to do and how to do it. Their objectives were spelled out for them.

3) Plans and policies were formulated by senior people and passed on to employees by their immediate superiors.

4) Information was confined to senior levels, and most of it

SECOND LIST

1) Much information flowed across the organization, short-circuiting official channels, and cutting across departmental boundaries.

2) People were encouraged to set their own objectives and develop their own methods of work.

3) There was consultation at all levels and full participation in the formulation of plans and policies.

4) Information was widely circulated to people at all levels.

was kept secret and confidential.

5) Most decisions were made by people in senior positions.

5) A large number of decisions were made close to the action by the people involved at lower levels.

6) Conformity, deference, and obedience, were the dominant characteristics of employees.

6) Innovation, creativity, and commitment to objectives were the dominating characteristics of employees.

7) Employees usually told top people what they thought they wanted to hear.

7) Employees at all levels often told top people unpleasant truths.

8) Punishment and threats of punishment were not uncommon. Rewards were few and infrequent.

8) Rewards were based on pre-determined results and were frequently given. (Non-economic as well as economic rewards).

9) Plans were formal, rigidly adhered to, and nobody questioned anything.

9) Plans were flexible and employees constantly strived to improve things. They asked a lot of questions.

10) Evaluations, promotions, and salaries were kept secret. Personality traits were important. TYPICAL WHEN BOSSES RUN THE SHOW.

10) Evaluations were openly discussed with employees with the emphasis on work performed and possible improvements. TYPICAL WHEN LEADERS RUN THE SHOW.

Chapter 2

Citizens or Subjects?

"Those who make peaceful revolution impossible make violent revolution inevitable." The words are those of John F. Kennedy. While we might not think so, they apply right now, to the Canadian Workplace. Employee revolts have produced a condition of shock in Bosses across the land.

Thousands of Canadians feel frustrated in their daily work because they are subjected to many forms of dictatorship. Have you ever taken a look at the rules and regulations that govern the lives of employees in most organizations? Sometimes there are dozens of them, usually in very small print. Employee *benefits* are often spelled out in large print. Usually, what the big print permits, the small print prohibits.

When you stop to think about it, every organization is a form of government in which every employee would rather be a citizen than a subject.

Leaders encourage their employees to become citizens. Bosses prefer subjects. Obedient subjects.

More and more people at all levels of society, Indians, Eskimos, students, housewives, people on welfare, the unemployed, the RCMP, medical patients, consumers, to name but a few, are demanding a voice and the right to have a say in regulating their own affairs.

How come? During the last ten years or so, more and more people have been receiving more and more education. The time has come to reap the harvest of education and that means more and more people are now seeking an opportunity to use their education in their daily work.

Sad but true, there are more dumb jobs today than there are dumb people. That's why so many educated people are unemployed. Underemployment is a greater problem in our society than unemployment. We are wasting human talent.

In a democracy, rulers rule by consent of the governed. Every company is a form of government and more and more employees would like a say in making the rules that govern them on the job.

Once upon a time, the rule of thumb for ruling workers was work hard, obey orders, and we'll take care of you. Al Capone used these rules for his employees. He meant *every* word!

If democracy is going to survive in Canada, then democracy at work must become a reality for Canadian employees across the land. Most employees want more control over their immediate environment and to feel that their work and they themselves are important. Employees don't want Bosses. They want Leaders.

Chapter 3

How Bosses Began

Human beings spent more than a million years in caves. Memories of those ancient times are deeply etched on our nervous system. Inside each one of us is a pre-historic man or woman ready for flight or fight if suddenly roused. The guy who could batter the brains out of friend and foe alike if his will was challenged was the Boss. But in a relatively short time we have evolved from caveman to spaceman and the need for Bosses has changed into the need for Leaders. Bosses are dominated by their inheritance from the past; Leaders are dominated by their concern for the future.

In primitive society the "Old Man" of the tribe was respected because he was old and he had managed to stay alive. The immediate post-cave society was dominated by Bosses who were cunning. Brute strength was replaced by crude intelligence. The Old Man knew more than other members of the tribe and his word became law. As tribes evolved and developed the Old Men became priests or kings. Still later, trusted servants were given the authority to manage other people. Those who did so wisely, got results. Often they were great but unsung Leaders. Those who did not know how to manage people wisely became tyrants, the precursors of Bosses. If they did get results it was at a fantastic cost in terms of human misery and human lives.

A thousand years ago a man was born either a slave or a Boss of some kind. He didn't have too much choice in those days. The Ancient Romans built an Empire with whips and slaves. Today these methods are not open to us. Today, in the 1970's, we have neither slaves nor whips, but Bosses are not convinced.

Let's take a look at the history of management for a moment. Roughly speaking it divides into five major phases:

1) Savagery   — Primitive
2) Slavery   — Ancient
3) Paternalism   — Feudal
4) Boss — Servant — Industrial
5) Leader — Team   — Democratic

After a long period of savagery and slavery management became paternalistic in the sense that fathers taught their sons how to manage land, crops, and herds. The Feudal Lords were paternalistic toward their serfs, protecting them in time of war, and collecting most of their crops in times of peace. Today many organizations still are paternalistic towards their employees. In return, they expect no waves.

With the advent of the Industrial Revolution and the movement from the land to the cities, management evolved into what is called the Boss-servant pattern. The distinction between the two was very clear and rigidly enforced by custom and by law.

25

Have you hired any servants lately? Of course not. Where have all the servants gone? Wherever they went, they went a long time ago. What have we got left? That's a good question. Stop and think about the relationship that you enjoy, or suffer, with your employers or employees. Is it paternalistic? or Boss-servant? It may be easy or difficult for you to describe where you are, but most Bosses are a mixture of 3 and 4, whereas Leaders are moving in the direction of democratic management, characterised by co-equal status for employees in terms of opportunities to make decisions in their day-to-day work.

It's no wonder that Bosses are confused, uncertain, and running scared. We have covered a lot of ground in a relatively short time. In 1903 the Wright Brothers managed to fly 103 feet above the ground — for 12 seconds. Only 787 months later Man went to the Moon.

Lunar landings, space probes, increasing populations, pollution, and diminishing natural resources, have created a fantastic range of possibilities in ways of living and raise urgent questions in the areas of religion, law, human relations, and management. Bosses are having a tough time unlearning old ideas about management but until they do, there is no way they will become more effective in dealing with employees.

"To be or not to be," that is the question for Bosses. Will they be big enough and bold enough to break through the bottlenecks and barriers that inhibit the exercise of leadership in management? Or will they continue to rail defensively and issue flat statements of eternal truth from the Holy Grail of History?

Bernard Shaw once observed that the reasonable

26

man adapts himself to the world, while the unreason-
able man persists in adapting the world to himself.
Bosses never stop trying to adapt the world to themselves. They try to create the illusion that they know
everything. They seldom succeed. But, unfortunately, the higher the Boss climbs the managerial
ladder, the nearer he thinks he is getting to the truth,
the whole truth, and nothing but the truth . . . so help
him God. And God help any employee who does not
bow down and worship him in the name of the great
managerial trinity: Tradition, Apathy, and Ignorance. Think about it. If you are a Boss, you have a
great future behind you.

Chapter 4

How Moses Went From Boss to Leader

Bosses try to do too much themselves; they don't delegate and then they have problems. People problems.

Jethro, who was Moses' father-in-law is often referred to in management courses as the first management consultant ever recorded.

EXODUS 18: 13-24

On the morrow Moses sat to judge the people, and the people stood about Moses from morning till evening. When Moses' father-in-law saw all that he was doing for the people, he said, "What is this that you are doing for the people? Why do you sit alone, and all the people stand about you from morning till evening?" And Moses said to his father-in-law, "Because the people come to me to inquire of God: when they have a dispute, they come to me and I decide between a man and his neighbour, and I make them know the statutes of God and his decisions." Moses' father-in-law said to him, "What you are doing is not good. You and the people with you will wear yourselves out, for the thing is too heavy for you; you are not able to perform it alone. Listen now to my voice; I will give you counsel, and God be with you. You shall

28

represent the people before God, and bring their cases to God; and you shall teach them the statutes and the decisions, and make them know the way in which they must walk and what they must do. Moreover choose able men from all the people, such as fear God, men who are trustworthy and who hate a bribe; and place such men over the people as rulers of thousands, of hundreds, of fifties, and of tens. And let them judge the people at all times; every great matter they shall bring to you, but any small matter they shall decide themselves; so it will be easier for you, and they will bear the burden with you. If you do this, and God commands you, then you will be able to endure.

Leaders have followed Jethro's advice for centuries, and have endured.

Chapter 5

The Boss Stops Here

Let's assume you're a manager, and you're busy. Your phone is ringing, and your secretary has gone downstairs for a cup of coffee. Suddenly there is a knock at your door. You look up: there's Joe Blow, a guy you rarely see, except out of the corner of your eye. He works down in the basement as a cleaner . . . or something. You ask him what he wants and he says, "Can I talk to you about my job?"

To set the scene further: the Personnel office is just down the corridor, and you are not Joe's supervisor. Joe, in fact, has bypassed two levels of management in coming to see you. Sure, you could try to pass the buck, refer him back to his supervisor, turn him over to personnel, or just tell him to go to hell. But what does this say about you? Why do you think Joe has come to see *you*?

Let's suppose you say something like "OK, come in and sit down, I'll be with you in a minute." So Joe comes in — looking pretty uptight, and sits down. You deal with the phone and when you're through you turn to Joe and say: "OK, what can I do for you?"

You have a hunch you might learn something from him.

Then Joe lets it all hang out. He says angrily: "I should have got that promotion last month."

Right or wrong, Joe thinks he's been given the gears. How come his supervisor hasn't been able to handle this matter with Joe? What does Personnel know, or not know about it?

If you don't listen to Joe, you will miss an opportunity to learn something about the way your department is working; or not working. If you were the manager in this situation and you got rid of Joe without listening to his problem, I'd say you were one hell of a Boss.

Chapter 6

Vital Needs in the World of Work

Some time ago I was asked to solve a problem in a large factory in Toronto which had resulted in a walk-out. I bought a sandwich and a coffee and joined the operators who were sprawled out on a grassy bank at the back of the plant. Quite informally, I asked them to tell me about the problem. They told me. Then I asked them for the solution. They gave it to me. I wrote it up almost word for word and presented it to top management. They thought the proposed solution was great.

All I had done was tell them what they already knew. The operators had already told several of their immediate Bosses how the problem could be solved, but their Bosses were not listening. If that sounds incredible, I can assure you this story in different forms could be repeated ad-infinitum across Canada. And we wonder why people are frustrated? This sort of thing is more common at lower levels of management which are thickly populated by Bosses. It denies some very basic human needs which assorted behavioral scientists and all kinds of consultants have been shouting from the roof tops for years now. Few Bosses ever listen.

SECURITY

1) All human beings have a deep-seated need for safety and security. I guess that's not hard to understand.

BELONGING

2) All human beings need to belong to a group in which they find acceptance. Few employees can resist this need.

SELF-RESPECT

3) All human beings need to feel they have something of value to offer to others, otherwise they feel useless.

ACHIEVEMENT

4) All human beings need to feel they are making progress towards a worthwhile goal. They need to achieve and be recognized for their achievements.

Now it's true there may be some people who don't feel these needs as strongly as others, but we all have them and research shows that the satisfaction of these needs in the world-of-work is very important to most employees.

Workers at the several automotive plants, for example, have demanded "meaningful work". They have suggested that instead of doing repetitive work on an assembly line, they should be allowed to move along the assembly line in groups and build a whole car. What does an assembly worker tell his kids when they ask him what he does for a living? He can't say, "I build cars." All he can say is "I tighten eight different bolts, eight thousand times a day." He rarely sees the finished product! A far cry from the satisfaction experienced by craftsmen in days gone by when they created some object start to finish.

As I see it, the challenge to Bosses is to learn how to inject the needed "vitamins" into the daily diet of work and keep employees alive mentally and emotionally. First requirement is for Information and Involvement. If you have tapped as many grapevines as I have, you would know that most employees are starved for information. They don't know what the hell is going on around them; they don't know why certain procedures are instituted or cancelled; and they are never involved in making decisions that affect them in a very intimate way on the job.

Recognition for a job well done is another necessary "vitamin". When was the last time your Boss praised you for something you did? You probably can't remember. When was the last time your Boss came over and asked you what he could do to help you do a better job? Probably never. When was the last time you did either for the people who work for you? But what a difference it would make. And damn it, why not? It doesn't cost anything; it sure helps to reduce tension and conflict on the job. Any job.

Senator H. Carl Goldenberg, Canada's leading expert in industrial relations and a famous labor adjudicator, has said many times that employers and unions should co-operate in making work more interesting. Unfortunately, I think there are Bosses in unions as well as in management, and too often they

34

reject the idea of close co-operation with management in looking at new ways of designing work to meet human needs. They are out of step with the vast changes taking place in most industrialized countries, where collaboration between management and labor results in sharing operational decisions on a day-to-day basis.

For example, in Sweden and West Germany all firms are required by law to have employee representatives on their boards of directors. No one has to be reminded that Sweden and West Germany are the two most successful countries in Europe, in terms of productivity and performance. The record shows that for every 48 days lost by workers in Germany because of strikes, Canadian workers lost 930 days.

Charles J. Connaghan, author of Labour Canada's report on labor relations in West Germany, stresses the need for better communications between employer and employees in Canada. He recommends that representatives of Labor, Government, and Business get together on a regular basis and review the economic facts of life. The existence of this report indicates a growing awareness of the need for leadership in meeting the needs of employees beyond the level of safety and security. Connaghan reports that German workers have a very definite say in setting hours, checking working conditions, lay-offs, and the economic welfare of their companies. "In effect," he says, "the average worker has been given a psychological stake in his company."[1]

You may recall that in August of 1976 150,000 construction workers in Quebec went out on strike, not for money, but for privileges. The same month, tradesmen in Vancouver walked out because of a dis-

35

agreement over parking payments. So often what seems like a minor issue is really just the tip of an iceberg; it may well reflect deeper issues that have been on the boil for months, maybe years.

Once during a strike I approached the men on a picket line and asked them why they were on strike. They replied, "The Boss will not listen to us." That is an expensive strike for all concerned.

A senior manager in a large bus company complained bitterly that he was having difficulty in filling jobs for drivers and other workers. "What we need," he said, "is a damn good depression. Then the workers will know who is Boss, and they won't turn up their noses at split shifts and dirty jobs." Quite a few Bosses have voiced the same sentiments. They think that in a severe depression employees will be less choosy about work and less inclined to demand rights and privileges. "*Then* we will manage them the way we have *always* managed them," Bosses reason. They are wrong. People have changed and they won't accept any attempts to frustrate their expectations.

A Boss in Edmonton a couple of years ago told me that he put the fear of God into his workers. (He, presumably, was "God".) He couldn't understand why he was having so many problems. After all, he was paying the best rates in town. In due course, he quit, and left for the Yukon. Another manager took over. On his particular shift, he visits each worker and chats with him or her about their work, about their families; about sport, what have you. The other managers visit their workers too, but they talk mainly about the importance of getting out the work and the need for better production. The new manager turns out more and better work than any other manager in the whole plant, and he has done this for nearly two years. The other managers sometimes have a tough time meeting their quotas. Don't get me wrong. They are very efficient in what they do: they are good Bosses. But the new manager is a good Leader. He knows how to meet the needs of his people.

A shift worker from an automotive plant told me that he had refused a promotion because all new foremen are told not to be friendly with the workers. "Your job is to work the hell out of them" he was told. This attitude is not uncommon among Bosses in any kind of organization.

I am not suggesting that employee needs can be met simply by good human relations. Too often the argument is heard that if somehow we can improve human relations we can solve our problems with people. This is putting the cart before the horse. If we improve the design of work, and the ways in which people can assume responsibility and experience achievement, we won't have to worry, because "good human relations" are the product of meaningful work in a supportive but challenging environment.

"ACTING" ON THE JOB

Let's assume your people have been well trained and have good experience in doing their work. How do you expect them to act on the job?

1)   ACT ON THEIR OWN?
                 or
2)   ACT, THEN CHECK WITH YOU?
                 or
3)   CHECK WITH YOU FIRST, THEN ACT?

or
4)   ASK YOU WHAT TO DO?
or
5)   WAIT TO BE TOLD?

LEADERS WANT PEOPLE TO ACT ON THEIR
OWN, MOST OF THE TIME. THEY EXPECT
PEOPLE TO MANAGE THEMSELVES.

HOW DO YOU EXPECT YOUR
PEOPLE TO ACT?

YOU ARE PROBABLY GETTING
WHAT YOU EXPECT
NO MORE, NO LESS.
THINK IT OVER!

1. Connaghan, Chas. J. Partnership – or Marriage of Convenience, Labour
Canada Official Report, 1976.

Chapter 7

Why Bosses Can't "Motivate"

More myths have been written about "Motivating" people than any other management topic. Bosses can't "motivate" anyone. Neither can Leaders. Why? The reason is simple: the only time people aren't motivated is when they are six feet under. People are motivated all the time because they are always trying to achieve something.

What is "motivation"? Bosses get a kick out of talking about what motivates other people, but they will seldom admit that the same things motivate them.

Once upon a time, a worker coming off night shift took a short cut through a graveyard to get home a bit earlier. He was a bit scared of graveyards, but on this particular night the moon was up, and he took a chance. Nothing happened. The next night the moon was up again. He walked through, and nothing happened. On the third night it was pitch dark but his fears had gone, so he started to walk through the graveyard again. Suddenly, he fell into a huge freshly dug grave for two people. Very upset, he struggled like mad to get out, but as he was a very short man he found he couldn't. Shaking like a leaf, he settled down into the far side of the grave and waited for help to come. About twenty minutes later, another man fell into the grave on the opposite side from the first man. He was even smaller than the other man so he too struggled to escape without success. The first man thought to himself, "I should tell that guy to keep still and wait till morning." He leaned across the grave in the dark and tapped the second man on the shoulder. "You can't get out" he yelled. But the little man did.

That story is one way to explain motivation. The trouble is that it does not help us to understand what "motivation" is, in a useful way. There are many perfectly respectable scientific definitions of motivation, but they are not much help to managers who want to "motivate" employees.

Bosses wind up using some variation of the carrot-and-stick approach to motivation. "If you do this, I'll give you something you will like." "If you don't do this, I'll give you something you *won't* like." This system gets very limited results because employees will use their energy and ingenuity to do as little for as much as they can get.

Leaders know that high expectation leads to high performance. They try to create not "motivation", but self-motivation. Rather than "control" workers they prefer arranging work in such a way that workers can control themselves. Leaders understand that everyone is always trying to become more like the picture they have of themselves in their mind's eye. Self-image is important. Anything that will enhance the image people have of themselves creates self-motivation. What do people want?They want self-respect, a feeling of importance, and to be valued for what they have to offer. To be worthless in our society means that you have nothing of value to offer. Leaders know what their people have to offer in terms of their individual differences, strengths, interests, and skills.

To create an environment for maximum self-motivation, Leaders pay special attention to four major items.

1) Non-verbal factors in their daily relationships with employees. Why? Because actions speak louder than words, or, "What you are speaks so loud, I cannot hear what you say."

2) Leaders provide feedback on how people are doing so that they can regulate and monitor their own performance.

3) Leaders provide generous amounts of information about the job they are doing.

4) Leaders make sure that people know what is expected of them before they start doing a job. Any job.

Leaders know that most people can be self-starters. Not many people like being told what to do and how to do it all of the time. Most employees prefer to work for themselves. They don't really want to work for you or for me. Leaders design work so that employees can manage themselves, they become self-motivated.

A Boss strives to get people to meet his needs. He calls this "motivation".

A Leader identifies the needs of his people and makes opportunities for them to meet their needs. This creates self-motivation.

Bosses strangle opportunities for achievement. Leaders feed opportunities for achievement. They know that people feel happier when they are doing their best. When this happens we are looking at an operational definition of high morale.

Chapter 8

Managers' Motivation Check List

Check off five of the following factors that you think influence you the most, and then tick off the five factors that you think have the most influence on your employees.

1) INTERESTING WORK
2) IMPORTANT WORK
3) INVOLVED IN MAKING DECISIONS
4) KNOWING WHAT YOU ARE EXPECTED TO DO
5) OPPORTUNITY FOR ADVANCEMENT
6) RECOGNITION FOR A JOB WELL DONE
7) WAGES, SALARY, OR BONUS
8) FEAR OF PUNISHMENT
9) WORKING AS A TEAM
10) GETTING INFORMATION YOU NEED

If you find there is a big difference between the two lists . . . you are a Boss. If there is no difference between what you have on your two lists . . . then you are a Leader. All people have the same basic needs.

At a certain level of income money ceases to be a motivator because other things become more important. I am not saying money is not important because you certainly can't do much without it. It's the way Bosses use money to "motivate" people that bothers me. They believe in rewarding people by taking a year to pay them an increase that was deserved last year. Do you reward your plumber, your dentist, or your lawyer? Of course not. You pay for performance. Employers should pay employees an increase in a lump sum, if they deserve one at all. Why not pay the increase in a lump sum at the beginning of the year, instead of at the end of the year. That way, employees could do something substantial with the extra money, if they want to.[1]

There has been a lot of research and argument about the influence of heredity and environment in the make-up of human beings. It has been said that if heredity loads the gun, environment pulls the trigger. In working with employees Bosses pull the trigger without first checking to see how the gun is loaded. They take an unnecessary risk. Leaders check carefully to see how their guns are loaded, and they get their people to pull the triggers only when they have taught them to take a very clear aim.

This is the difference between "motivation" and self-motivation. Leaders know that when employees don't know where they are going, any road will get them there. Bosses don't worry too much about their destination, they are too busy "motivating" their people to be busy.

1. Bull, Warren, "Compensation Managers, — Let's Not Sleepwalk the 70's," Business Quarterly, Winter 1973.

Chapter 9

"Magic" is Murder in Management

For many years Bosses have been bamboozled by three magic words:

PLANNING

ORGANIZING

CONTROLLING

These three words are supposed to describe what managers spend their time doing, and Bosses often talk about how hard they work at one or the other of these alleged managerial functions. Baloney.

Bosses arc not the only ones who have been hypnotized by managerial magic. The real culprits are educators and consultants who make a living perpetuating these paralysing myths.

Any casual observer with half an eye can see that very little if any of a manager's time is spent on planning, organizing, and controlling. Most of it is spent rushing about performing ceremonial rituals, gathering and passing on information, making decisions, and communicating.[1]

If Bosses are going to learn how to be Leaders it is

up to management educators to put the brakes on all this mystique about management in the abstract, and start helping Bosses to solve the everyday problems of management. Bosses need to learn managerial skills on the job, not a whole bunch of management theories away from the job in totally unrealistic surroundings. Mind you, it's very nice to get a break from the old sweat-shop to go to one of these courses, but it won't make much of a contribution to leadership skills.

Anyone can pick up a bagful of management concepts at any psychological supermarket but it won't help them to become a Leader. Canada's billion dollar bash in education over the past few years has produced a surplus of people with degrees and advanced degrees. But it has not produced a surplus of Leaders in management for the world-of-work.

Bosses pay the most extravagant lip-service to the cliches of good management, but when the chips are down, reveal themselves for what they are.

For example, one Boss who thought he was a great Leader told all of his people to settle their own problems and differences of opinion before they got together with him. Sounds good? He didn't want to listen to a lot of opinions, no sir, all he wanted from his people were the facts, the whole facts, and nothing but the facts! After I sat in on a couple of his meetings and talked privately with some of his staff, I found out that on a number of occasions he was never informed of some rattling good ideas because they were based on opinions.

Management has been described as the Art of Arts because it requires the co-ordination of talent to achieve a vision. You might be an outstanding solo performer in your field, and that's fine. But once you become a manager you have to get results through others. I have always preferred the idea that management is the art and science of meeting planned objectives through the efforts of others. But, if you think of a vision as an objective that you can only achieve through the efforts of others, then, in a sense it can be described as an art. When you are put in charge of a group of people in factory, office, church, home, volunteer group, or what have you, make no mistake about it, you are a manager. You are expected to get some results from whatever the group is going to do. Whether you turn out to be a Boss or a Leader will depend on what you have learned about leadership. Maybe the only kind of manager you ever had was the Boss kind. That's bad.

You can learn to be a Leader, but not from books. Books can give you some suggestions that may be helpful, but the only way to learn leadership is on the job. If you work for a Leader, you will learn from the way he gets you to do things for him. He will expect a lot from you but he will give you a free hand with no threats.

Bosses have a dry, drab, and mechanistic notion of their role as managers. They have very little confidence in the ability of their people to manage themselves and as a result they do a lot of things they should get other people to do. That's why Bosses work hard, not smart. Uninspired, they fail to inspire. Yet more than anything, employees need inspiration. Some room for hope that things will be better tomorrow than they are to-day. A belief that they will be able to do more tomorrow than they are doing to-day, and a real conviction that they will be more as human-beings than they are to-day. Leaders know the magic of inspiration and they know how to apply it. Bosses are victims of "Planning", "Organizing" and "Controlling".

1. See H. Mintzberg, The Manager's Job Folklore & Fact, Harvard Business Review, July August 1975.

Chapter 10

Memo to the Boss

Dear Boss:

1) Please discuss with us the results you want us to achieve.

2) Please agree with us on how we will measure the results we achieve.

3) Please give us the authority and responsibility to manage ourselves.

4) Please review our progress regularly with us.

5) Please update your personnel policies and bring them in line with our needs.

6) Please maintain a continuous and free flow of information from you to us about important issues that affect us.

7) Please work with us to create a climate for individual as well as corporate growth so that we may grow, achieve, gain recognition and compensation for good results.

Chapter 11

Let Your People Grow

In the right environment people will grow. How do you go about creating the right environment for growing people? Bosses practise the Jungle theory which is very simple and very dramatic. They just throw people into jobs and let them sink or swim. This encourages the survival of the slickest. Leaders practise a kinder method. They let their people grow up. Bosses keep their people down.

Bosses love "little" people and they breed them by the barrel-full. It's easy, all they have to do is to keep on running around and getting involved in doing things that other people are paid to do. They love to spend hours debating washroom facilities, parking and space priorities. If a passion for these kinds of activities happens to be your pet perversion, all I can say is lay off and watch your people grow. They will sure as hell surprise you.

I remember talking with a senior Boss at a big insurance company during a staff walk-out. He told me he had been amazed that his secretary was able to operate a computerized unit. "Even I don't know how to do that," he said. I asked him why he was amazed and he said, "She's only a secretary." See what I mean? A secretary is a secretary, a carpenter is a carpenter, a cleaner is a cleaner, and that's it — according to Bosses. They get what they expect, and very little more.

To sharpen the focus on growing people, let's take a look at a couple of diagrams, adapted from Transactional Analysis that show how Bosses and Leaders relate to employees.[1]

"Boss"	Employee	Leader	Employee
Parent	Parent	Parent	Parent
Adult	Adult	Adult ⟷	Adult
Child	↖ Child	Child	Child

In this scheme of things you will see that if you are a Boss, you are enjoying a parent-child relationship with your people. They, however, are far from enjoying it.

If you are a Leader you are relating to your people on an adult-to-adult basis. Both you and your people are not only enjoying your relationship, you are finding it to be mutually rewarding.

The first step in this whole business of being a Leader is to figure out where you are in your present dealings with employees. All a Boss has to do to start the ball rolling is to get down off his high horse and listen to what his people are saying. Of course, if they aren't saying anything he will have to spend some time and patience in convincing them that he is for real.

Credibility is a big factor here. Don't rush it, and don't overdo it. I once knew a Boss whose people thought he was sick, or something, when he said he wanted to hear their opinions. Leadership is strong medicine, an overdose on a Boss-hardened worker can knock him for a loop. Build on success, one step at a time. Properly handled this approach to getting people involved will work wonders.

Common sense is not very common, but it doesn't take too much savvy to realize that if employees become more effective and more productive, the whole outfit is going to benefit.

A shift in emphasis from Boss to Leader can be explained by showing how Leaders look beyond money as the only motivator in the traditional sense.

BOSSES EMPHASIZE	*LEADERS EMPHASIZE*
Effort	Results
Control	Self-control
Competition	Collaboration

In helping employees to grow in the world-of-work, it's what Bosses and Leaders believe about their people that makes the difference in the results they get.

I visit companies where management gives more attention to the needs of machines than it ever dreams of giving to employees. Human beings are infinitely more complex than machines and need constant attention if they are going to grow. In cases where jobs are very repetitive it is easier for a Boss to automate the whole operation, but because it is so expensive he can't afford to do it. Then he has to live with problems. People problems.

Dishwashing, for example. Any Boss will tell you there is nothing, but nothing that can be done about improving a dishwasher's job. I was told so by the head of a large hospital cafeteria in Ontario a few years ago. There were all kinds of problems in this cafeteria: dishes were broken frequently, turnover was high, and absenteeism was common. I talked with some of the staff who operated the dishwashing equipment and got them to tell me their side of the problem.

It boiled down to this: they felt like big fat zeros. If you know anything about hospitals you will know that in a hospital dining room the doctors will sit in their section, nurses their section, maintenance people in their section, and so on. These dishwashers sat under a stairway in the dark. They were treated, quite unconsciously, as the least of the least.

The director was a very pleasant person but she did not realize she was acting like a Boss. I asked if washing dishes is an important job. Of course it is. All the food in a hospital passes over the plates that are washed in the dishwashing department.

The director said "Yes, the job is very important."

Then I asked: "Then why don't the dishwashers *know* their job is important?"

The director was quite unaware that the dishwashers were starving psychologically. However, she was still certain that nothing could be done.

I asked her who checked the bacterial content of the water each day, and I was told that someone in the lab looked after that. I asked if dishwashers could be trained to do this themselves because it would give them more responsibility and make the job more interesting.

"Impossible," she said. Special training would be required.

To cut a long story short, two of the dishwashers were enrolled in an evening course for lab technicians, and the others took it in turns to assist the lab technicians. A story was put into the hospital bulletin about the importance of washing dishes together with a picture of each dishwasher in the section. Result? Turnover stopped, absenteeism went down almost a hundred per cent, there were fewer breakages, and the dishwashers now know the importance of their job. They also have a table of their own in the staff dining room, right next to a window.

I will admit that helping people grow is sometimes a tricky business, and it helps to brush up on your knowledge of human needs and what makes people tick. I don't put much stock on books as a solution for Bosses, but I recommend them as a point of departure. They help to agitate the cortical cells. The best books on management contain a lot of useful and interesting examples of what has happened, good and bad, in a variety of settings where leadership skills have been applied. If you are a Boss, look through one or two. If you don't think you are a Boss, read them anyway. You may learn something. Most Leaders have gained from research and experience. They are alive to needs for growth.

Bosses complain bitterly to me about the dummies they have working for them, and if they can't seduce their understanding they are more than willing to rape their attention. After they get through with their strong arm stuff they are still beefing about results. I tell them that because people grow, jobs must grow. What is the point in giving people more and more education and allowing them to do less and less.

If you are a Boss and think all this stuff is for the birds, I have news for you. Your people are giving themselves raises you know nothing about. In fact, the biggest raises your employees ever get are the ones they give themselves. Don't believe me? OK, how does this grab you? Any time you fail to feed your people what they need to grow on the job, all they have to do is withdraw 25% of their interest and their effort. That's how they can get a 25% increase in their pay. Get it? They do!

FREE TEST FOR "INFORMATION"

Can your employees answer these questions?
1) What is the cost of the product you make?
2) What is the cost of the machine you work with?
3) What is your reject rate?
4) What would it cost to stop your machine for two hours?

If they don't know the answers, you have no excuse. You are a Boss.

THIS IS WHAT HAPPENS WHEN	*THIS IS WHAT HAPPENS WHEN*
BOSSES	*LEADERS*
Don't trust their people	Trust their people
Don't involve them in decisions	Get them involved in decisions
Don't communicate	Communicate regularly
Don't share responsibilities	Share responsibilities
Don't share credit	Share credit
Don't provide opportunities	Provide many opportunities
Don't give recognition	Give full recognition

IN RETURN *THEY RECEIVE*	*IN RETURN* *THEY RECEIVE*
Very little loyalty Poor performance Conflict and complaints	A lot of loyalty Good performance Little conflict and few complaints
Low productivity High costs	High productivity Low costs

WHY?	*WHY?*
Because they offer meaningless work	Because they offer meaningful work
They believe in authority	They believe in participation
They believe in obedience and compliance	Because they believe in initiative
Because they do not enable people to integrate personal goals with organizational goals	Because they enable people to integrate personal goals with organizational goals
They operate in parent child relationships	They operate in adult-adult relationships
They manage by activities	They manage by objectives
They emphasize procedures and routines	They encourage creativity and innovation

They believe that money is the only motivator and tend to starve other important needs

They know that money is not the only motivator They feed other equally important needs

If you are a Boss . . . Start moving in this direction ⟶

1. *Berne Eric*, Games People Play, *Ballantine Books, 1964.*

Chapter 12

Up Your Perishing Pyramid

Believe it or not, in West Germany there is one Boss sitting on top of a pyramid, literally. His company offices are built in the shape of a pyramid and each floor is equated with a level of management status, the idea presumably being that employees will be motivated to rise to a higher level in the pyramid.

A lot of Bosses go to extremes to motivate employees but this particular Boss must be unique.

Conceptually, any organization can be depicted as a pyramid: the President, Chairman, Director, or whatever, is at the top. All the lesser lights are located at descending levels of importance, but each one sits on top of a pyramid within a pyramid. Each of these pyramids is governed by either a Boss or a Leader. When there are more Bosses than Leaders the going is rough and results are poor and far below potential.

Bosses at all levels of any organization devote years to the art of climbing pyramids, and there isn't much they won't do to get to the top. Bosses achieve success as climbers, but seldom as Leaders.

To get a grip on this once potent but increasingly

impotent concept, we need to understand that we have inherited most of what we know about "management" from two giant pyramids of power: the Church and the Military. In both of these structures, authority once ruled supreme. Disobedience, almost unheard of, was rewarded with either execution or excommunication. No one questioned authority.

For more than two hundred years the Church and the Military provided models for almost every other organization. Up until the last fifty or sixty years, that made a lot of sense in that the average churchgoer, citizen, or soldier was uneducated and depended on orders from the top of the pyramid. Only at the higher levels were there educated people. The "lower orders" had to be told what to do, and how to do it.

No more. Inside church and military organizations, revolt in the ranks, rebellions, and uprisings of all kinds are occuring. The lower orders are demanding a say in what goes on that affects them.

The pyramid represents the traditional picture of the organization in which every function is spelled out to the letter. Every job description is rigidly defined, and charts with neat straight lines portray little boxes in which people are supposed to work. Conformity, stability, continuity and efficiency. It all looks beautiful on paper. But it's a lie. Bosses don't know it. Leaders do.

Bosses see their pyramid this way:

They see planners at the top, and doers at the bottom, but ne'er the twain shall meet. This set-up guarantees organizational-schizophrenia, and creates alienation between the planners and doers. Another thing: if anything goes wrong, the doers delegate responsibility upwards. Because they were not involved in the planning, they can't be blamed.

Leaders know that decisions must be made at the lowest levels of the pyramid. Employees at these levels know more about what is going on there than anyone else and, given information and responsibility, they can stretch, grow, and start to manage themselves.

Leaders know that planning and doing must be integrated at all levels of an organization to improve performance and productivity. Planners and doers don't necessarily have to get married, but they must learn to live together in common-law.

The pyramid concept creates the illusion that one man at the top has all the genius required to run a complex structure. This is not true, of course, and perceptive Leaders are beginning to recognize the facts and do something about it. When the President of Sears Roebuck walks into any one of his nine hundred stores, there are only three levels of management between him and the lowest employee: the store manager, and the first line supervisors. Flattening the organization pyramid frees up communication and gets more people involved in doing more things.

If you have problems in your pyramid caused by Bosses, rigid structures, endless divisions and subdivisions of work, the only cure is convert Bosses into Leaders, loosen up the structures, and group and consolidate the work into meaningful modules.

Do you know who can do that best? The people doing the work, that's who. All they need is a mandate and a deadline. Put the key people in a room for three days and tell them to redesign the organization chart for maximum effectiveness. What they come up with in three days or less will startle you. Why? Because they can't fool each other. That's why. They know who is making a contribution and who isn't. I have seen a complete level of supervision eliminated by this process. Result? Better performance and higher production. Try it. It works!

You must have heard about "Pyramid Power". All kinds of people are buying those little plastic pyramids, or the large ones made of wire. Apparently there is a mysterious form of energy released in the lower third of any pyramid with a hollow structure, provided it is aligned with the magnetic north. Razor blades are supposed to sharpen themselves and pieces of raw meat do not decay. In Egypt, scientists are investigating the mysterious energy found only in the lower third of the original pyramids. They claim that it defies all known laws of science.

At the same time, management scientists in the West are performing complex research into the most effective ways of harnessing human energy in the lower third of organizational pyramids. They too have made dramatic discoveries that are now being applied by Leaders in the world-of-work. Bosses are sceptical about these discoveries whenever they hear about them. Bosses are not willing to experiment and they are reluctant to change.

Chapter 13

Don't Let Your Schooling . . .

Mark Twain said he never let his schooling interfere with his education. Bosses do. Leaders don't.

Says Peter Drucker "There is no reason to believe that the diploma certifies too much more than that the holder has sat for a long time."[1]

Before the year 1500, Europe was producing books at a rate of 1000 titles per year. By 1950, Europe was producing 120,000 titles a year. By 1960, just ten years later, the output of books on a world scale approached 1000 titles per day. Today, scientific, technical, and management books increase at a rate of some 60,000,000 pages a year.[2] Bertrand Russell used to say that as we continue to learn more and more about less and less there is a danger we may end up knowing everything about nothing.

Bosses are schooled. Leaders are educated. Education has nothing to do with schools. The best that schools can provide is vocational training for a union ticket.

Alfred Whitehead, the great philosopher, once

wrote that an educated person is not merely a well-informed person, "Such a person is the most useless bore on God's earth."

Regardless of their schooling, Leaders are flexible and probing in their thinking. They are able to think in terms of interdependence, process and relations. When they deal with people they focus on dynamics, not mechanics. They know that the goal of all learning is to keep on learning. They may not know all of the answers, but they certainly know all of the questions. And questions are keys that unlock doors. Doors of insight and perception.

Bosses are convergent closed-mind thinkers because they jump to conclusions and then look for evidence to confirm them. They want only the facts, they don't want to hear opinions. Leaders are divergent thinkers because they look at many possibilities before they reach a conclusion. They want to hear opinions before they assess the facts.

Bosses are primarily vertical thinkers, they emphasize facts, logic, and judgment in terms of "how many of these expensive machines can we buy with X $?" Leaders are vertical and lateral thinkers, because they emphasize creativity and innovation as well as judgment and logic in terms of "in what other ways could we get the results we want without using these expensive machines?"

Paul Getty, the world's richest man, who was once a roughneck on the Texas oil fields, is on record as saying that "formal business education is no guarantee that a person can step forth into the business world qualified to manage as much as a candy store." In a similar vein, Peter Drucker has written that, "we need to punch big holes in the diploma curtain through which the able and ambitious can move."

To the typical Boss in medieval times knowledge was "salvation", and by knowledge he meant knowledge of eternal principles handed down from the past coupled with unshakable faith and rigid conviction.

The typical Boss in the 19th Century thought of knowledge as power. And by knowledge he meant more "facts". Facts were more important than opinions. Every time.

To the enlightened leader of the 1970's, knowledge is freedom, and by freedom he means knowledge of knowledge as well as facts. He knows too well what Marshall McLuhan meant when he said that today people learn far more out of school than they ever learn inside.

I am not saying that Bosses are not intelligent, very often they are. The trouble is that very often they love machines but hate people. Brilliant technical Bosses wind up as brilliant failures because technical knowledge can't be applied to people.

Brilliant Bosses are a pain because they think they ought to know everything about everything and this encourages them to pass judgment on a variety of things about which they know little, or are grossly misinformed.

The net result is that people give up trying and cease to use initiative. "What's the use?" they say.

The difference between unsuccessful Bosses and successful Leaders at any level is that Bosses are focused on efficiency and Leaders are focused on effectiveness.

Regardless of education, Bosses are not sure where

64

they are going or what they are trying to do. Regardless of education, Leaders always know their objectives and have plans outlined to meet them.

Leadership theories do not help Bosses to become Leaders. Too many organizations waste their money buying programs on theory when they should have been investing in programs designed to develop leadership skills right on the job. This can be done, and is being done, and is far more effective in terms of results. This is not schooling, it is "hands on" education that enables managers to perform in actual situations which allow feedback and follow-up.

Too often a graduate in management theory winds up in a staff position. Although he has learned a lot about "management" he has not necessarily learned how to manage.

Many effective managers often find themselves bossed by management theorists who drive them to distraction. They either find another job, or wait until it becomes obvious that the theorist is unable to deliver.

Invest in These Books and Grow

Douglas McGregor	*The Human Side of Enterprise*
Robert Townsend	*Up the Organization*
Alvin Toffler	*Future Shock*
Fred Herzberg	*Work and the Nature of Man*
Peter Drucker	*Management*
Peter Drucker	*The Effective Executive*

Saul Gellerman	*Motivation and Productivity*
Koontz & O'Donnell	*Principles of Management*
Anthony Jay	*Management & Machiavelli*
Rensis Likert	*The Human Organization*
Abram Maslow	*Eupsychian Management*
Special Task Force Report U.S.A. to Secretary of Health, Welfare & Education	*Work in America*
M. Scott Myers	*Every Employee A Manager*
William F. Keefe	*Listen, Management*
George Odiorne	*Management by Objectives*
David McLelland	*The Achieving Society*

1. *Drucker, Peter,* Age of Discontinuity, *Harper Row, 1969, p 131.*
2. *Toffler, Alvin,* Future Shock, *Random House 1970.*

Chapter 14

Bosses Can't Communicate

On a day-to-day basis what would you say is the single most important aspect of an employee's environment? Not too sure? Imagine that you arrive at work one day and as you walk into the building you see the Boss, the Big Banana, or whatever you call him walking towards you down the main corridor. As you pass him you say "Good morning", grunt, say "Hi", or whatever. The Boss completely ignores you, he doesn't say a word, and walks right on. How do you feel?

During the morning you pass the Boss again on the way to the John. You smile, nod, and try to mumble something, but still the Boss ignores you. How will you feel for the rest of the day? Puzzled? uneasy? insecure? Probably all three.

On a day-to-day basis, the most important part of an employee's working environment is the attitude the Boss communicates. This attitude is communicated either verbally or non-verbally and creates the emotional climate in which employees either live or die, psychologically. Managers cannot choose not to communicate. They do it all the time in order to get things done through other people.

Studies by Paul T. Rankin in 1929 and others since that time show that between 70 and 80% of a manager's time is spent in communication. It breaks down this way:

9% in writing
16% in reading
30% in talking
45% in listening

Most people learn how to talk from their parents and they learn to read and write in school. But where do they learn to listen? For managers this is a critical question, because they spend about 45% of their time in the listening process. How do they listen, what do they hear? Leaders understand the listening process. Bosses don't listen, they only hear what is being said. They suffer from Wishful Hearing. Very often they can't wait to hear what they are going to say next.

Many grievances that wind up in arbitration start with a front-line Boss who does not know how to listen. Leaders know that listening is not hearing. They know that the art of listening lies in the art of letting people talk with themselves. This is ancient wisdom. Psychiatrists are paid up to $100 per hour to help people listen to themselves. Your great-great-grandmother knew this, and so did mine.

The accelerating rate of change in our daily lives makes it difficult to concentrate on listening as a healing process. But that is what it is. If you are a manager or supervisor, think back to the time when an employee came to you and poured out a problem. If you are a Boss you were probably embarrassed, not knowing what to say. Perhaps you spent a fair bit of time making what consultants call "NSES". Non-specific encouraging sounds. "Ah ha", "Hmm," "I see", and so forth. Perhaps you drummed your fingers on the desk, or looked sideways out of the window, wondering how you could get out of the situation. It's possible the employee will thank you for your help and leave you wondering what happened.

If you had really understood what was happening, you might have been able to provide much greater assistance through effective "listening". In this kind of situation, most Bosses don't listen at all, they tell the employee what to do and how to go about doing it. Very often this kind of Boss has a real need to be needed. They can't resist the parent-child relationship. What happens? If the employee takes the advice, and things don't work out, who gets the blame? The Boss. Another result is that the employee starts to depend on the Boss for advice whenever he has a problem. Leaders avoid a dependency relationship with their people like the plague.

Communication is the management skill most frequently used and abused by Bosses in their efforts to get things done through others, and yet it is the one subject on which management and employees tend to agree. Whenever I ask an employee what makes a manager a Leader, he will say something to the effect that you can talk to a Leader and he will understand. Remember, Leaders listen nine times more than they talk, and they ask three times as many questions as they give answers.

Listening helps a Leader compare the doubt in people's minds with the conviction in their voices. Bosses are afraid to listen because the other guy might be right, and they might have to admit that they are wrong. Bosses think that listening is a sign of weakness rather than a sign of strength. Leaders know that through listening they learn much that will help them to help people achieve objectives. They are focused on getting people to talk about the things that are preventing them from doing a better job.

Bosses are DOGmatic and CATegorical in their statements about people and then they wonder why they are living a CAT and DOG life with them. Verbal hygiene is the basic requirement of an effective manager but very few comprehend the fantastic influence of language on human behaviour. For example: "I enjoyed meeting you" can be interpreted in many ways, depending on the non-verbal dimension.

Research on the non-verbal aspects of communication reveal that about 60% of a verbal communication is communicated at the non-verbal level. Without the non-verbal dimension, words would have no meaning.

Bosses say things like *should, ought, must, never, always.* These words imply perfect knowledge and perfect control which, of course, is just not possible. Leaders use words like *prefer, like, more convenient,* and *appropriate,* because the words help to create a better emotional climate. They know that effective communication depends more on getting people to listen, than on what is said to them. If people are turned off before you say a word, they won't hear anything.

Have you ever heard a Boss giving instructions to an employee? After he has given his instructions, he will probably say something like this: "Did you understand what I said?" What is the employee going to answer? Ninety-nine times out of a hundred he is going to say "yes." If he says he doesn't understand the Boss might think or say he is a dummy. So very often employees will tell lies because they are afraid to tell the truth. What kind of climate are they living in? The moment the Boss has turned his back they rush over to the nearest person and say "What did he mean"?

When Leaders give instructions they try to find out what the employee is going to do before he does it. They will ask the employee to tell them what he is going to do, now he has heard the request, or the instructions. It takes a little longer, but it saves a lot of time, strife, and money in the long run.

If you are a Boss, language will use you, and you won't even know it. If you are a Leader, you will be aware of the unspoken assumptions implicit in the structure of language, and you will use language effectively. Leaders know that human understanding is achieved not when John understands Bill according to John's way of life, but according to Bill's way. When Bosses listen they listen only to themselves.

Millions of dollars have been wasted trying to communicate from top down in organizations. Upward communication is blocked because employees pass up only what they think the Bosses want to hear. When information is heavily filtered on the way up and heavily amplified on the way down, the stage is set for communications chaos.

Bosses interview their employees from behind a desk and don't realize what that does to communication. At the non-verbal level it may communicate many things. Insecurity . . . "I am the Boss", or "Know your place". These non-verbal barriers to effective and full communication are removed by Leaders. They sit with an employee or employees where each can see the other in a pattern of partnership, rather than Boss and subordinate. Try pushing your desk up to the wall so that when someone comes in to see you, all you have to do is turn around and face them. You will be agreeably surprised at the difference in the way employees will respond. They will appreciate it, and eventually, so will you.

Chapter 15

Performing on the Job

Judgment Day comes once a year for Bosses and employees alike in the guise of performance appraisal. At no other time in the year is there such a general gnashing of teeth and plucking of hair. Appraising performance makes Bosses more uncomfortable than anything else they do. Bosses know how to discipline people. That's simple. Just bawl them out or get rid of them. But performance appraisal, that's different. That's tricky. When it comes to figuring out what a person has or has not accomplished during the past year, most Bosses become as nervous as a nudist climbing through a barbed wire fence.

Because they don't know what else to do, Bosses act like old-fashioned judges in a court-room drama. The indictment is drawn up in the shape of a long list of deficiencies to which the accused employee is not supposed to plead guilty or not guilty. Just guilty. After pleading guilty, he is supposed to accept whatever sentence is handed down because Bosses know best what is needed to improve performance. Some Bosses like to play their favorite record: "I am Just

Trying to Help You."

Leaders don't play records, and they don't play games. They expect all employees to know how they are doing, at all times. Not just once a year.

The difference between a Leader and a Boss in conducting a performance appraisal is this: Bosses tell their employees how they are doing. Leaders don't. Instead, their employees tell them. They can do this because the employees are constantly monitoring their own performance based on objectives and standards mutually agreed upon.

A fact of life in the world-of-work is that many employees only find out how they are doing when they are being fired by a Boss. Then the Boss spells it out and lays it on the line. "You did not do this" or "You did not do that." The employee is completely bewildered because this is the first time he has ever been told what was expected of him.

I wish I could remember how many times employees have said to me, "I don't really know what I am expected to do around here." It usually turns out that their Boss doesn't know either, or else he is too busy being busy. Leaders don't have this problem because they sit down with their people and explain what is required of them ahead of time.

How is your performance — in performance appraisal? Are you an old fashioned judge? Or are you an up-to-date Leader?

Bosses grade jobs as though they were grading eggs. Once a job is graded, classified, signed, and sealed, it is not supposed to change. Result: Bosses end up walking on eggshells and get egg on their faces. Jobs can't be graded like eggs because they change all the time. They change all the time because the people

74

in them are all different. Some will do more than others. Bosses have a Procrustean attitude towards their people; they make them fit jobs, instead of making jobs that fit people. Bosses who grade all jobs, and set all salaries, will have plenty of problems.

Leaders don't have to be told that some of their people are more valuable than others. They know. They match the nature of their people with the nature of their jobs.

If you are a Boss striving to be a Leader, try a new approach. Instead of presenting your employees with a long laundry list of activities or duties to perform, or fulfill, get agreement with them on what constitutes their major responsibilities. Alongside each responsibility outline the results that you both agree should be achieved when the responsibility is properly carried out. Then employees know what they have to do and how to measure their results. Review with them from time-to-time, or if responsibilities change.

Responsibilities	*Results Required*
1	1 ....
2	2 ....
3	3 ....
4	4 ....

Chapter 16

Beware The Boss

The influence of a Boss extends far beyond the office, factory, or wherever he works. Every day his employees take his influence home to their families, to their neighbours, and to their communities.

Canadian Mental Health Specialists stress the need for leadership in the world-of-work in terms of providing employees with a friendly supportive climate to work in. Thousands of Canadians are immigrants cut off from friends and relatives and often have no one to talk to in times of stress. This is one reason why maybe one out of every three hospital beds is filled with people who are emotionally sick.

Because a Boss is strong willed, and insensitive to people, he will almost certainly cause tension and emotional problems for some of his people. His failure to show leadership in creating a healthy emotional climate at work will reduce productivity and return on assets. It will also affect the development of his employees as responsible citizens.

Satisfying work is a basic human need because it contributes to self-respect. But the way most work is structured for millions of workers today creates mental and physical problems, family instability, delinquency, drug and alcohol addiction. Leaders are doing something about the way jobs are designed. Bosses are not.

Bosses cause a deadly fall-out of verbal and non-verbal bacteria which infects employees with multiple symptoms of mental and physical sickness. This includes depression, withdrawal, boredom, absenteeism, and sabotage. Employees die on the job because their daily diet of work is lacking in the psychological "vitamins" required to keep them alive and growing. Leaders know how to enrich the daily work of their people. Bosses don't. Bosses don't even know that people are psychologically starving to death right under their noses, while they pontificate "People are our most important asset" or words to that effect.

It works the other way around, too. As far as I know, the Death Wish has never been identified as an active force in any organization. But it's there. "Dear Boss . . . drop dead" is the painful message aching its way up every organization. When Bosses drop dead on the job it's usually explained away by saying, "he worked too hard" or "he couldn't relax." Any African witch doctor knows better. The intense drop dead attitude of many employees to-day is the equivalent of that old black magic known as "pointing the bone."

Employees who actively wish the Boss would drop dead create a climate of tension. Verbally and non-verbally, employees cast a deadly spell on the Boss. The total effect is emotional pollution and poor performance. The Boss tries to overcome this by what he likes to call "corrective action". This usually makes

77

things worse. The Boss thinks he controls his employees. In fact, they control him.

There is a plant which specializes in making parts for the auto-industry. During a tour of this plant I was told by a worried Boss that he was experiencing a morale problem. We walked through rows of giant punch press machines which made a deafening noise as the operators stamped out metal parts. Each operator wore protective goggles, and a special set of ear mufflers to keep out noise. Each operator was chained to his machine by what are known as pull-guards. These chains automatically pull back the arms of the workers after each descent of the giant stamper.

The operators could not communicate with one another in any way except by signs. To do their work they had to insert a piece of metal, step on a pedal and wait for the stamp to descend. Easy work. No thought required. Just ideal for robots' movements: pick up metal, insert metal, step on foot bar, withdraw metal part.

The Boss told me he couldn't understand why he had a morale problem because he was paying top rates and the workers had everything they could possibly need. Good canteen, good benefits and medical plan, good pension plan, good recreational facilities. When I asked him why he hadn't introduced automation to solve the morale problem, he replied "Money. Too much money."

Chapter 17

On Mind Expansion

More than 2000 years ago Aristotle wrote that a fly has eight legs. For hundreds of years scholars accepted without question until one day someone questioned Aristotle's authority and found that a fly has only six legs.

We have lived more than 50% of the 70's but Bosses are still looking in the rear view mirror of the 50's and 60's. They do not innovate; they do not question.

Our survival as a nation with a viable economy depends on creative thinking, and creative thinking depends on questions about things that most Bosses take for granted. Bosses must learn to unlearn old ideas.

A Leader knows that his greatest virtue, aside from ignorance, is curiosity. Questions can be more important than answers. Most bosses don't like questions, particularly questions about questions. Claude Bissell, former President of University of Toronto, summed up the need in these words, "We need minds that will not respond mechanically and instantaneously to emotional catchwords, they will have the imagination to grasp the consequences of events, the boldness to break the log jam of routine."

It has been said that Man may be an unsuccessful experiment in curiosity. Because of their enormous power over Man and his resources, creative managers are our only hope if the experiment of Man is to continue. Is there a method that can help Bosses to become Leaders in solving problems? Behavioral scientists think there is. They have suggested that all our actions may be viewed as part of an effort to solve a problem, or to communicate something, or both. The scientific method has for too long been associated with men in white coats, slide rules, and laboratories. In reality, the "method" is a very effective way by which Leaders adapt to problems and consists of careful observation, accurate description and classification. Are you a good observer? How many squares can you see?

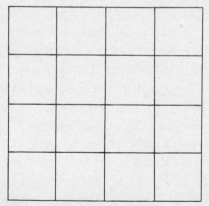

What gets Bosses into trouble is not what they don't know, it's what they know that isn't so. If you can't see more than 16 squares you are probably a Boss. Leaders see 160 or more. British philosopher Robin Skynner says that most people do not consciously operate on assumptions. They operate on beliefs. They do not treat the views they inherit tentatively, sceptically, as temporary pictures built up when less information was available. They treat them as established facts, self-evident traits, unquestionable dogmas, true for all time. By doing so they automatically prevent themselves from individually learning anything further.

It has been said that the words curiosity and creativity have an interesting relationship — they both begin with C and end with Y. C = "see", Y = "why".[1] Leaders see why. Bosses don't. How many squares do you see now? The more you look the more you see: as your perception changes, so will your behaviour. You won't tell someone they are "stupid" if they "see" more than you do.

To the curious and the creative, failure can be a stepping stone to success. Leaders never cease to be curious. In Management by Objectives, of which more later, Managers are encouraged to set at least one creative objective each year. They undertake to achieve something never before attempted in their department. It must be desirable, attainable, time-bounded, measurable and creative.

Try this experiment: write down your full legal name and time yourself. Now repeat the process, only this time, leave out every other letter. Now compare the time in each case. Why did it take you twice as long to do half as much work? Habit. How do you raise your right arm? Well, how do you? We take a lot for granted without a single question.

Because Bosses look only for *good* ideas, they overlook ideas that might be highly effective in solving problems simply because they are strange or different. Bosses have been amazed to see what creative ideas can emerge in a brief brain storming session with a group of colleages during a seminar. There are acres of proof in terms of cash results to justify encouraging creativity among employees.

The whole world is crying out for things to be improved. Bosses must become Leaders in creativity to answer this demand. They must learn how to do more with less. This is the challenge of the 70's. There is always a better way to do anything, if we have the courage to try. Fear of being judged wrong or having our ideas described as ridiculous or impossible is a powerful brake on creativity.

Alexander Graham Bell was called an idiot. He invented the telephone. Westinghouse proposed to stop a railroad train with wind. He was ridiculed. Goodyear was laughed at by everyone as he worked for eleven years to vulcanize rubber. Not long after World War II top scientists derided the notion of accurate inter-continental missiles. As late as the 1950's people were saying that space travel is impossible.

Leaders know that employees don't have to learn to be creative; they are creative. They have been taught to ignore their creativity under Bosses, at home, and in school.

An army captain once was asked why one of his men stood at attention throughout military exercise. "Because that is his job" the Boss captain replied. The captain did not know why the man was involved in the exercise. Research showed that the man's job was to hold the horses. It is this lack of imagination, this unquestioning attitude, that makes Bosses breed invisible horses, and give them to visible men to look after.[2]

1. McLelland, David C. & David Winter; *Motivating Economic Achievement*, Free Press, 1969.
2. Jay, Antony, *Management & Machiavelli*, Pelican 1967, p 99.

Chapter 18

MBO . . . Dead or Alive?

Every manager has heard about Management By Objectives, but few can explain what it means, and fewer still can claim to have practised it successfully. No system of management has aroused such interest and controversy, which is rather surprising considering that in one form or another it has been around for at least 15 million years, and has proved itself to be a highly effective system for human survival.

MBO was the rage in the 1950's and 60's, but now, in the 1970's, a number of Bosses are busy trying to bury their mistakes and blame them on Management By Objectives. "It takes up too much time", "too much paper work", "it just doesn't work", or, "MBO is out of date" are typical comments of Bosses who have never understood, let alone practised MBO. But if MBO is no longer relevant, what is the alternative? Is it management *without* objectives? When Bosses say they have tried MBO, what they really mean is that they have tried either Management by Objections, or perhaps Management by Obsession, but never Management by Objectives.

MBO, as a philosophy or as a way of life completely eludes the comprehension of Bosses. MBO is nothing more than the conscious direction of actions towards goals, in such a way that all employees are enabled to monitor and manage their progress towards clearly defined objectives.

The fastest way to find out how an organization is being managed is to ask employees how they know when they are doing a good job. If at all times they know how they are doing, they are managing and being managed by objectives. If they don't know, (often the case), or if they are not sure, they are being managed by activities.

Management by Activities is the hallmark of Bosses at work. Under MBA everybody is busy being busy, working very hard, and trying to do things right. Everything has been "planned", "organized", and "controlled", right down to the last detail. The illusion of progress hangs heavy in the air. On closer examination, however, the perceptive observer becomes aware that although people are doing things right, they are not doing the right things.

In other words, MBA confuses efficiency with effectiveness because Bosses focus on activities rather than results. Bosses love to tell me how busy their people are, but when I ask them what results they are getting, they look puzzled and say "excuse me, I am busy, I have to go." And off they go, spinning their wheels faster than ever, and getting deeper and deeper into more and more activities.

At a very primitive level, MBO has been around since the dawn of history, and if you want proof of that, all you have to do is to compare the behaviour of Primitive Man with the behaviour of Civilized Man.

You will find that Primitive Man practised MBO long before it became a game that Bosses play. He hunted in a clearly defined physical territory, and he always knew what his objectives were. They were very simple and very basic: Food, Safety, and Survival, in that order. The tribal hunter always knew when he had achieved his objectives; his stomach was full, he was safe, and the tribal unit was still intact. Civilized Man has something in common with Primitive Man. Civilized Man is also a hunter; he is out hunting, trying to "bring home the bacon" in one way or another, to meet his needs for status, as well as survival.

There is, however, one very significant difference: Civilized Man hunts in a different kind of territory; a territory that is, in fact, an area of responsibility which is rarely well defined. This is why employees so often say "I don't really know where I am, or where I am going in this organization." They are genuinely lost and cut off from a basic need to know where they are, where they are heading, and what progress they are making. Hunting to achieve poorly defined objectives in poorly defined areas of responsibility puts a tremendous strain on the survival mechanism of employees, because most employees genuinely want to do a good job in order to satisfy their needs for achievement. The larger the organization, the more frustrating and confusing the situation becomes to Bosses and employees alike.

Managing by Objectives is a way of managing which involves employees in making decisions and setting objectives. It has been described as a philosophy as well as a method because it is based on some deep assumptions about the nature of human beings.

In one of the best selling books on management of

all time, *The Human Side of Enterprise*,[1] Douglas McGregor outlined these assumptions in terms of his famous Theory X and Theory Y. Under X, managers make assumptions about employees in negative terms: they don't want to work; they are lazy; they must be checked, threatened and controlled. In effect, they are Bosses. Under Theory Y, McGregor said, there are managers who make different kinds of assumptions about their people: most people want to work, and most people do not need to be controlled or threatened in order to make them work. In effect, they are leaders. Managers who operate primarily under Theory X assumptions usually get less favorable results than managers who operate primarily under Theory Y assumptions.

The term "Management by Objectives" was first mentioned by Peter Drucker in his book *The Practice of Management*,[2] published in 1954. He strongly emphasised team work with team members committed to common goals.

Under Leaders, Management by Objectives enables employees to practise self-management because it provides more responsibility, freedom, accountability, and it encourages self-control, and self-evaluation. The implications of MBO are deep and dramatic in terms of creating a democratic system that reduces the power and authority of Bosses and shares them with employees. The reason that so many companies have failed with MBO is very simple: too many Bosses have used the system as another form of control and another way of imposing their objectives on people. "Here are my objectives, now tell me how you are going to achieve them", or "Here are my objectives, achieve them or else." Mind you, for some employees just knowing what the Boss's objectives are would be a vast improvement on total ignorance, but it is still a far cry from achieving the maximum return on human potential that is always available when properly tapped.

When these basically Theory X approaches fail to get quick results Bosses are quick to take refuge in some caustic criticism of the system, and brand it as a failure along with other fads that have come their way. There is nothing wrong with MBO. It is the most basic, logical, biological, and psychologically satisfying way to manage, or be managed, because it takes care of fundamental human needs.

Whatever your job, whether it is making radios, selling insurance policies, tending the sick, or pounding the beat, it is carried out in some kind of organization that is trying to achieve a purpose. If each employee is to do his best he must at least know what is expected of him and his efforts must be focused on a common objective. Without objectives clearly defined at all levels employees become confused, frightened, and very often demoralised.

The alternative to managing by objectives would appear to be managing without objectives, and strangely enough there are many Bosses who prefer to manage without objectives because it makes no demands on them in terms of leadership. They don't have to worry about listening to people, getting them involved, or finding out where they could make a real contribution to the enterprise. All they have to do is to make sure people work hard, keep them busy, threaten, punish, reward, drive. That's all they know.

Management by Surprise is their forte; moving from crisis to crisis is their delight, and although they would never admit it, they enjoy it. They are up front and centre with lots of little people running in all directions asking what to do, and how best to do it. It's great. For Bosses.

Effectively managing by objectives simply means that everyone in an organization is clear on what they have to do in order to attain mutually desirable objectives. There are many variations on this fundamental theme of managing by objectives, but this is the essence of them all. Funny thing, many Bosses will swear up and down that they are using objectives, and yet, I have never found one that could produce a clear operational statement of his objectives. Leaders can.

MBO or MBA?

WHICH SYSTEM ARE YOU USING?

UNDER MBA
A boss says his job is running a company, a department, or a store.

UNDER MBO
A leader says his job is to meet specific objectives that will contribute to the overall goals of his organization.

UNDER MBA
Bosses emphasize EFFORT.

UNDER MBO
Leaders emphasize RESULTS.

UNDER MBA	UNDER MBO
Employees have different and unclear perceptions of goals.	Employees have similar and clear perceptions of goals.

RESULT	RESULT
Friction, Conflict, Confusion, Chaos, People busy being busy, spinning their wheels, and getting nowhere *FAST*.	All of its members can be attracted into a cohesive pattern through leadership and involvement in setting goals. Another way of expressing this is by saying that the wheels of a car must all move in the same direction.

1. McGregor, Douglas. The Human Side of Enterprise, McGraw Hill 1960.
2. Drucker, Peter. The Practice of Management, McGraw Hill 1954.

Chapter 19

Punishment or Discipline?

Are discipline and punishment one and the same? Managers who are Bosses usually think so. Managers who are Leaders however, usually equate discipline with education.

Bosses are very sensitive to mistakes and errors made by their employees, but they are not very sensitive to the abilities and achievements of those same employees. When it comes to taking corrective action with employees, they are lost. Let's see what you would do in the following situation:

Bill Bates is the supervisor of ten clerical employees at The Wallpaper Corporation in Eastern Ontario. One day he is approached by several of his employees complaining somewhat bitterly that one of their co-workers, Joe Jones, is getting to them in the worst way. They say that Joe is sloppy, dirty, untidy, and often late. They want Bill Bates to do something about this situation pretty darn fast. They have had more than enough of Joe's peccadillos.

Bill Bates has been aware of Joe's behaviour for some time now, and he has been putting off what he regards as a difficult and unpleasant task.

OK, assume that you are Bill Bates, what would you do in this situation, and how would you do it. What would you actually say to Joe? Would you think this through step by step carefully, before you talked with Joe — or would you get him into the office and just get mad at him?

In all probability a Boss would call Joe into his office and try to change his behaviour by saying something like this: "Joe you'd better smarten up, or else". At best, this kind of approach would produce reluctant conformity, or it could produce hostility and become a personal issue between supervisor and employee.

On the other hand, a Leader might call Joe into his office with the objective of getting Joe to change his own behaviour. He might say something like this: "Joe, are you aware that your behaviour is disturbing some of the people in this office?"

At this point, the Leader is endeavouring to establish whether Joe does in fact know that he is causing a problem. Very often, I have discovered, employees are quite unaware of these things. If this is all news to Joe, the Leader proceeds to "educate" him on the facts, perhaps in the following manner:

"Some of the people around here, Joe, see you as an untidy person, sloppy, dirty, and often late. I want you to understand that these things don't bother me too much, personally, because I don't see you that often, and your work is satisfactory." Here, the Leader avoids locking horns with Joe and prevents the matter from becoming a personal issue between them. He might continue in this fashion:

"Do you want the other people around here to see you as untidy, sloppy, dirty, and unpunctual?"

Here the Leader tries to get Joe to acknowledge that he, like most employees, does not want his work group to see him in negative terms. If Joe says he couldn't care less, and that he is quitting, your problem is solved. But if Joe indicates, no matter how reluctantly, that he definitely does not want to be poorly regarded by his group, the Leader might continue by saying something like this:

"All right Joe, if you really mean that you do not want your colleagues to see you as that kind of person, what are you prepared to do about it?"

At this point, the Leader does not *tell* Joe what to do . . . he *asks* him. He puts the onus on Joe to decide for himself what he is going to do. In other words, he is going to get Joe to change his own behavior. The reason for this is that Joe is far more likely to follow through on his own decision. If a Boss tells him "Do this or else," his behavior may or may not change.

Note that asking questions rather than giving answers is a much more effective technique in this kind of situation. The old rule of listening nine times more than you talk, and asking three times as many questions as you give answers, is very applicable in the disciplinary process.

If you look up the word "discipline" in Webster's Collegiate Dictionary, you will find that it means "to train or develop by instruction and exercise, especially in self-control."[1]

When the traditional manager hears the word discipline, he automatically thinks in terms of punishment. When a Leader in management hears the word discipline he automatically thinks in terms of his most important function: developing people to a standard of excellence in doing their work.

By self-control and self-management, I am not talking about some wishy-washy permissive philosophy. I am talking about the very essence of discipline as it has always been understood. When a Leader creates discipline in an organized group of employees, it means that they will do their work, and do it well, whether he is around or not. This is the meaning of self-control, self-management and self-discipline. Surely this is a worthy and vital objective for every manager at every level of an organization. Bosses reduce productivity and performance by continuously *checking, controlling*, and *supervising*, to make sure that people are doing exactly what they were told to do.

By doing this they are admitting, in effect, that they are incapable of creating discipline. When things go wrong and employees make mistakes, Bosses practise punishment.

The first step in the disciplinary process is not to bawl someone out because they have made a mistake. Instead it is to find out whether the person who made the mistake was properly instructed how to do the work required. If the instruction was faulty in any way, the person who made the mistake is not accountable and must be re-instructed by a competent instructor. If mistakes continue after proper instruction, then it is legitimate to reprimand the worker. If mistakes continue after a reprimand has been given, then, and only then, should more severe measures be considered. It is only at this point, that we are talking about something that could be described as *punishment*.

A lot of Bosses "see red" when they hear someone talking about "participative management" because they think it has something to do with being nice to people, or being soft. On the contrary, it is a discipline that enables a leader to harness the latent talent and energies of his people. It demands from Bosses a new and much deeper understanding of human behaviour. It demands, in fact, that Bosses mature from the traditional parent-child relationships they have formed with employees, to adult-to-adult relationships which release and reinforce the achievements of human beings.

Leaders encourage employees to learn from mistakes and challenge them to improve. They know that employees who fear taking risks will turn into minimum performers; they will play it safe. How could you go about challenging a group? Let's say a group of employees wants more control over setting the hours they work. A leader could say something like this: "Sure, if you produce x number of units for x number of weeks, you can have more control in setting your hours. If you can't produce, you can't have more control."

This approach challenges employees to practise self-management in order to achieve an objective that is important to them. Creating discipline in a work group of any kind depends upon many things. For example, does everyone in your organization, or department know clearly, and without equivocation, the exact time they are supposed to be at work, and ready to work, each and every day?

If you think this question is ridiculous, just try asking a few people where you work, and count up the number of different answers you get. I suspect the number will astonish you. Try it. The point is that if your people are not clear on simple matters, how much more likely is it that they are unclear on other matters of greater importance? All employees need to be clearly "instructed" if discipline is your objective.

Bosses trying to "discipline" employees have a tendency to tar all with the same brush. For example, a Boss might put a sign up in the shop or office that reads: "Anyone found drinking on company premises will be dismissed immediately." Will this help to create discipline in employees? Just because a couple of the 150 employees have been found drinking in the washroom during the last twelve months does not mean the other 148 are going to do the same, does it? If you want to create discipline and good morale, don't insult people. Bosses do it all the time and don't even realize they are doing it.

Do you punish your employees if they dare to disagree with you? Studies have shown that most managers think that disagreeing with a manager is a sign of disrespect. They also believed that the best way to handle difficult employees is to be tough and put the pressure on.

If your employees never disagree with you . . . you are a Boss.

1. *Webster Collegiate Dictionary, G. & C. Merriam Co., 1961.*

Chapter 20

What Would *You* Do?

Assume you are a first line supervisor in a large organization. You have been asked to replace another supervisor in a branch operation because he was unable to create "discipline". You have never met any of the staff at the branch office but you have heard about them through the grapevine. What you have heard does not exactly enthrall you in any way, and you realise they will be difficult to handle. The staff at the branch office has heard about you through the grapevine and they are not too happy about your taking over either. It seems that you have a reputation for "discipline".

You plan to meet the branch office staff at 8.30 a.m. in a staff lounge next Monday morning. There will be about twenty people present. How will you handle this situation? After you have said "Good morning", or whatever you say in the morning, what will be the very first thing you will say to this group? Think this over carefully, right now.

Perhaps you are thinking that different supervisors would handle this situation in different ways, and of course you are right. However, allowing for variations in style, language, and methods, supervisors generally behave either more like a Boss than a Leader, or more like a Leader than a Boss. A Boss in the above situation would probably lay it on the line . . . "I have heard all about you guys and from now on there will be no more nonsense or else."

Let me tell you what a real-life supervisor did in this situation. The first thing he said, after saying "Good morning", was something like this: "Coffee will arrive shortly. I am going to leave this room for fifteen minutes. While I am gone I want you to make a list of the three most important questions you would like to ask me. When I come back, I will do my best to answer your questions." He smiled, and left the room.

After fifteen minutes he came back to the lounge, and sure enough the group had come up with their three most important questions, and several more as well. The supervisor did his best to answer the questions, and once he said he did not know the answer, but that he would find out and let them know. After he had listened, he asked them to talk about some of the things they would like to do in their work, and in what ways he could help them to do a better job. They stayed in that lounge for three hours. There have been no more problems since this supervisor took over.

Let's analyse his strategy. First, he allowed the employees to make a list of the important things they wanted to know, in private. He made refreshments available. He listened carefully to their questions and answered them carefully. In this way he established credibility. He did not tell them anything until he

98

heard what they had to say. After they had got a few things off their chests, he asked them more questions so that he could identify their needs and learn how he could help them satisfy those needs. Now they were ready to listen to him. He knew that if he had tried to tell them what *he* wanted them to hear right at the start, — as most Bosses would have done, they would have heard what he said, but they would not have listened. He wanted them to listen and they did.

Chapter 21

Time-Tortured Bosses

When a Boss is tortured by Time — look out! He is going to create a lot of pain for a lot of people.

Bosses never have enough time, no matter how hard they work; they always fight a losing battle against the Tyranny of Time. If lack of time doesn't kill them outright, they usually wind up trying to kill time in a variety of ways, including booze.

The symptoms of Time-Tortured Bosses are well known and highly infectious:

The Time-Tortured Boss never delegates — he *knows* it's quicker to do it himself.

The Time-Tortured Boss makes snap decisions that result in snapping and snarling and, very often, unsnapping the original decision.

The Time-Tortured Boss talks 9 times more than he listens which means simply that, generally speaking, he is generally speaking.

The Time-Tortured Boss over-concentrates on details and loses the big picture. In other words, he can't see the woods for the trees.

The Time-Tortured Boss rarely asks any questions, he's too busy giving out answers.

Time-Tortured Bosses naturally create Time-Tortured Employees who are nervous and can't make decisions for themselves.

These employees suffer from boredom on the job, frustration and lack of interest. They never get a chance to show what they can do because the Boss is too busy doing it for them. The Time-Tortured Boss is out of step with the accelerating rate of change, and he can't figure out why he seems to have less and less time. He is not aware of Time as a dimension which he can consciously control. The result is that time controls him unmercifully. Peter Drucker sums up the situation in these words: "Time is the scarcest resource and unless it can be managed, nothing else can be managed."

All aboard the good Space Ship Earth are hurtling through the void on a fantastic trip through space and time.[1] There are no return tickets for anyone. As guardians of human and physical resources, managers have an awesome responsibility to see that all employees have a good trip when they give up the Time of their lives in order to work.

Employees working for Bosses find that time goes S L O W L Y, because it is boring and without challenge. On the other hand, employees working for Leaders find that time goes quickly, because their work is interesting, challenging, and full of achievement and recognition. The busy Boss is a busy "B". Business luncheons two and three times a week to "save time" and regular (too regular) staff meetings, both a waste of time. One Boss complained to me that he didn't know what he was going to say at his staff meeting; when I asked him why he was going to have a meeting he said: "because it's Thursday."

A Leader never gets caught in this trap. All are invited to attend his meetings when there is something important to discuss, but not all are expected to attend unless they have something to contribute. Everyone gets the minutes within 24 hours.

Meetings chaired by Bosses drag on for hours and people get tired, hot, and bored to death. Leaders provide a minimum of comfort for staff meetings. All they need is a flip chart stating the purpose of the meeting, an agenda circulated ahead of time, a deadline, and someone from another department to chair the meeting who knows absolutely nothing about the topics for discussion. His job is to manage the meeting, keep it on track, bring it to an end on time, leave everyone knowing what has been decided and who is going to do what in the future. This arrangement leaves the Leader free to participate in the discussion.

Some of the most effective meetings are held in a bare room with no tables, and no chairs. Coffee is served after the meeting. Usually, they begin at 11 a.m. and, curiously enough, they always seem to finish in time for lunch!

Have you noticed how often Bosses complain that there are only 24 hours in a day? They worry about the number of hours they put into their work. Leaders know that they have very little time each day to call their own. They worry much more about what they put into their time, than the amount of time they put into their work.

How can you do more in less time? It can be done by finding out what is important in your work, and concentrating your efforts in that area. For example: do you know which of your responsibilities are the most important? could you identify them and assign a priority to each of the first five?

I have seldom met a Boss who could answer these questions in the affirmative. Yet knowing the answers to these questions is an essential pre-requisite to effectiveness. A Boss once told me that the most important thing he did every morning was to open the mail. When I asked him why, he said: "Because many years ago, someone lost a cheque." This Boss, by the way, always answered his telephone. His secretary only answered the phone when he was out: he explained that his secretary, who had worked for him for nearly three years, might not know what to say.

A doctor I once knew did much the same thing in his office. After his secretary had left for home, he stayed behind, sometimes for several hours, to check all the bookings and the billings. He was worn out in a few years and finally he took a salaried job with an insurance company.

Bosses are nearly all victims of ABULIA. Know what that is? It is the persistent habit of doing pleasant things first, and unpleasant things last. Have you noticed? For example: they put off dealing with frustrated customers, or staff, until the situation reaches boiling point, and then they wonder why there is an explosion! Leaders know that the most effective time-saver in the English language is the word "NO"! They save valuable time by knowing what *not* to do.

An odd thing about Time is that Bosses always want more of it, and yet they already have all there is. In one respect Bosses and Leaders are alike, and like everyone else: we have exactly the same amount of time, no more, and no less. What is it that enables Leaders to use their time more effectively than Bosses? They invest time the way they invest money; in the place that brings the highest return on investment. A Boss is constantly preoccupied with how he is going to spend his money. A Leader is more concerned about how he is going to spend his time, because time is the most expensive resource of any organization.

How does a Leader *know* where to invest his time to get the highest return on his investment? A Leader invests most of his time in the 20% of his job that produces 80% of his results. This applies across the board to almost anyone who wants to maximize results. The question now is whether you know how to find the 20% of *your* job that produces 80% of your results? If you don't, you need help.

If you are a Leader, both you and your people *know* where they should be investing their time for maximum results. If you are a Boss, neither you nor your people will have the faintest idea. They will be investing a little bit of time here, and a little bit over there, but it will add up very little in the way of significant results. The fact is, and this is documented in many studies, productivity can jump 20% or more when time is invested effectively in high yield areas of responsibility.

Have you noticed how Bosses tend to judge people by the amount of time they spend on a project? Leaders on the other hand judge people on results, obtained by an agreed deadline.

If asked to give a talk about work to an outside group, a Boss will usually jump at the opportunity; a Leader is far more likely to recommend someone else on his staff as equally if not better qualified.

Bosses work in a state of constant crisis. A Leader

will postpone something *urgent* until tomorrow, so that he can do something *important* today. Because Leaders work on a long-term basis, they prefer to do important things today in order to prevent a crisis tomorrow. In contrast to leaders, Bosses work on a short-term basis, from day-to-day, hour-to-hour, and minute-to-minute. Do you know where your time goes? Saint Peter Drucker says: "If you think you know where most of your time is going, you probably don't know where any of it is going." Most Bosses know how to make up their financial budget, but when asked to make up their time budget, they don't know what to do. The most expensive resource is Time, and yet few Bosses know how to budget this precious commodity!

Leaders consciously budget their time. Every day they invest at least 15 minutes in making tomorrow happen by using the following plan: each day they write down in order of priority five important things that must be done the next day. When tomorrow comes, they start on number one, and work their way down the list. Of course they will be interrupted throughout the day, but if they follow this method they will be further ahead than if they did not. This is an old, tried and true method that was recommended to the President of Bethlehem Steel many years ago by Ivy Lee, a public relations man. Within five years its application helped turn Bethlehem Steel into the biggest independent steel producer in the world.

What do Leaders do to stay ahead of their Time? First, they keep in mind the axiom that nothing is easier than being busy, and nothing is more difficult than being effective. Secondly, they practise the following principles, which I call:

FIRST AID FOR TIME-TORTURED BOSSES

1) Find out where you are spending your time.
2) Stop doing unnecessary things. Learn to say NO.
3) Concentrate on essentials — the 20% of your job that produces 80% of results.
4) Set priorities.
5) Reduce time spent in Low Yield Areas.
6) Increase time spent in High Yield Areas.

If you follow these simple rules you can multiply your time effectiveness at least ten-fold.

1. See Dr. Derm Barrett's "Everyman's Guide to Time Maagement", Business Quarterly, Spring 1973.

Chapter 22

Stop Being a Boss, Start Being a Leader

If you are a Boss and you want to start being a Leader, there are several things you can do. You can talk over your situation with a reliable consultant who can help you to see yourself as your employees see you. It is dangerous to abruptly change your behaviour. Your employees will suspect something is wrong and this will arouse feelings of insecurity.

An effective consultant can help you to identify your management style by making a confidential and anonymous survey of your people, and analysing the results with you. Don't get mad and cancel out. Remember, your objective is to find out where, and in what way, your behaviour is affecting productivity. You will have to Stop, Look and Listen. Here are some guidelines on what to Stop and what to Start. The key here is to Adapt, rather than Adopt.

WHAT TO STOP	WHAT TO START
STOP looking into the rear view mirror. The past is gone.	START looking into the future — the only place where you can make anything happen — and ask yourself six basic questions: WHAT are my personal objectives; what am I trying to achieve? WHY am I trying to achieve the above objectives? WHEN will I attempt to meet the deadlines for these objectives? WHERE am I now in terms of accomplishments to date? HOW do I plan to achieve my objectives?

WHO among my friends can help me with advice. What group could I join that would be helpful with information?

STOP placing unnecessary barriers between yourself and your people. Whether you are a president or a first line supervisor, get out from behind that desk. A desk is a non-verbal barrier that inhibits communication at many levels. You don't need it unless you are feeling insecure and need all the props you can get.

START by moving your desk around to face the wall. When someone enters your office all you have to do is just swing around and face them, and greet them with a smile. You can read people better when you see all of them. In modern offices desks have disappeared and coffee tables have taken their place. If you need to write, a desk top pulls down, or slides out of a wall.

STOP trying to be perfect at everything you do. Nobody expects you to walk on water all the time.

START admitting that you can be fallible, and when you are in the wrong, say so. People will respect you for this more than you might think.

STOP trying to do everything because you can do it better and faster.

START to distinguish between what you alone can do and what you can get other people to do.

STOP asking for all of the facts before you make a decision. You can never get all the facts anyway. So why frustrate yourself and other people.

START by asking for opinions concerning whatever facts you have been able to gather. Facts are interpreted in the light of opinions.

STOP doing most of the talking most of the time.

START by listening nine times more than you talk, and asking three times as many questions as you give answers.

STOP assuming that most of your employees are lazy, don't want to work and need close supervision most of the time.

START assuming that most of your people do want to work, are not lazy, and do not need constant supervision. Give them Super-Vision.

STOP having meetings because it's Thursday.

START having your meetings only when you have something to discuss that is important. Let someone else manage the meeting.

STOP dumping work on people. This guarantees it will either not get done or it will be screwed up.

START getting people to accept new responsibilities by explaining what's in it for them. Not just money, but achievement, responsibility, opportunity for advancement, recognition.

STOP investing your time in activities with a low return on investment.

START by identifying the 20% of your job that produces 80% of the results. This is where you must invest most of your time, most of the time.

STOP resisting new ideas and developing a hardening of the categories.

START encouraging your people to brainstorm for new ideas when dealing with problems. '

STOP believing that what you look at is what you see. Especially when you are looking at employee behaviour.

START behaving as though what you look at is not what you see, but what you believe. Check your assumptions before you jump to conclusions.

STOP depending on bits of paper to manage things for you. You may be in love with paper, but your people hate it.

START remembering that the best management systems are invisible. You can't see them. They don't depend on forms. They depend on the ideas and attitudes of people.

STOP thinking vertically when you are trying to come up with a new idea.

START thinking laterally using free associations. Read Edward de Bono's books on Creative Management.[1]

STOP looking inwards and being introspective about your company or department.

START looking outwards at what is happening in other departments, other organizations, and in the community.

STOP telling people what to do, and how to do it. That's a parent — child relationship.

START encouraging people to manage themselves. Make them do their homework before they bring you their problems.

STOP trying to "motivate" people. You can't do it. People change, but you can't change them.

START by giving people an opportunity to gain recognition and real achievement in their work. From then on they will be self-motivated.

STOP hiring hands.

START looking at the whole person that comes with the "hands".

STOP tolerating poor and sloppy performance. Your people will lose their respect for you.

START by insisting on a standard of excellence. Tell people what you want and make no bones about your requirements.

STOP keeping your people down. A lot of little people walking small won't help you grow at all.

START helping your people to grow up and mature into accepting full sized responsibilities.

STOP spinning your wheels by confusing efficiency with effectiveness. Working harder and faster is no guarantee that you will get the results you are looking for. Efficient people are not effective unless they are doing the right things at the right time.

START getting real traction by focusing the efforts of your people on predetermined objectives clearly understood at all levels. People cannot achieve what they cannot define.

114

STOP managing by activities. That's hunting big game with a shotgun.

START managing by objectives. Hunt with a rifle. You'll get better results.

STOP acting like god, "master", "Boss", or the "old man". These labels have negative connotations and if your people label you in this manner, you may get negative results.

START acting like a Leader by getting your people involved in making decisions on their own. DO consult with them.

STOP acting like the all-knowing or aggrieved parent.

START acting like an adult dealing with adults.

STOP feeding your problems with time, energy, money, and other resources.

START feeding your opportunities; they are high yield areas for time investment.

STOP taking work home at night and weekends. You may be working hard, know a lot about your job and be very efficient. It won't help you to be effective.

START by making sure that people do not leave their problems with you for you to solve. This is monkey business. The care and feeding of

115

STOP rewarding people for their services. You don't reward your plumber, do you? Of course not. Employees don't think of themselves as being "rewarded" for their services.

monkeys is not your business. You should be on the golf course more often.

START thinking in terms of paying your employees for services rendered like everyone else. Pay for performance.

STOP judging people by how *busy* they are.

START judging people by the *Results* they are getting.

STOP keeping your great ideas to yourself.

START becoming a member of a team. Hard-nosed necessity to-day, in every organization, demands full membership in terms of involvement. Share your great ideas.

STOP saying it can't be done.

START saying there are many ways in which it could be done.

STOP saying "If only I had" . . . whatever it is you don't have . . . "IF" is a NO word — and no way for Leaders.

START by looking around to see what you can do with what you have. This is the acid test of you as a Leader. Leaders do more with the same amount, and very often they do more with less.

STOP reading endless reports and journals. Reading is something someone else can do.

START other people reading things for you. Employees can read and summarize articles you don't have time to read. They can identify what you should read from a whole mass of detail and bring this to your attention.

STOP dictating all of your letters, proof reading them, and signing all of them. Your time is too valuable.

START letting your secretary answer some of your mail and signing it. This way she can grow up, you can ease down.

STOP waiting for things to happen.

START making things happen. You must see yourself as a person whose responsibility it is to make something happen.

STOP trying to improve boring jobs with more money.

START building into those jobs some of the psychological vitamins that keep people stretching: recognition, responsibility, etc.

STOP trying to control
people all of the
time.

START getting people to
think in terms of
controlling
themselves so
that when you are
not around,
everything
carries on. This is
the real meaning
of discipline.

1. de Bono, Edward. *Lateral Thinking for Management*, AMA, New York.

Chapter 23

New Light on Organizations

Freud used to say that if you want to change a man's behaviour, you must first change his perception, then he will change his own behaviour. Try this little exercise and see if it will change your perception — and maybe your behaviour. Get a piece of scrap paper and draw an organization. Draw whatever comes into your mind when you think about the word "organization". You will probably draw something like this.

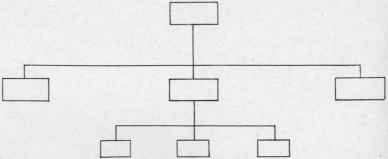

OK. This is the traditional way of looking at an organization. It won't help you do much about improving results, will it? Here's a more effective way of looking at organization:

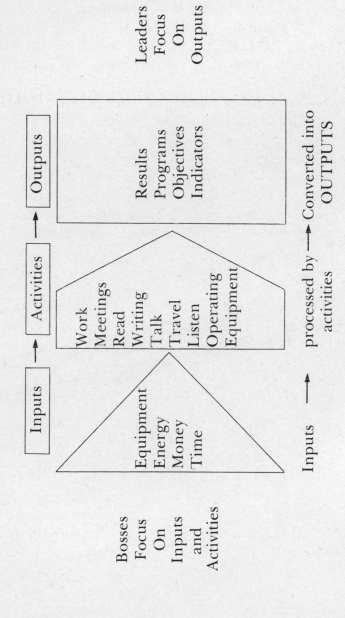

Inputs	Activities	Outputs

Inputs
Equipment
Energy
Money
Time

Activities
Work
Meetings
Read
Writing
Talk
Travel
Listen
Operating
Equipment

Outputs
Results
Programs
Objectives
Indicators

Bosses
Focus
On
Inputs
and
Activities

Leaders
Focus
On
Outputs

Inputs → processed by activities → Converted into OUTPUTS

Now if your perception has changed, you may be able to change your behaviour by cutting back on the deadly wheel-spinners that trap Bosses into working very hard and being very efficient.

Leaders are effective because they focus on outputs required before they worry about inputs and activities.

Don't try to stop being a Boss because you think you should. Start being a Leader by changing your perception of yourself. What is your role as a Leader? It is to help people grow and develop. It's a challenge to every Boss, but one that he can ignore only at the risk of conflict and chaos.

Leaders have learned how to make tomorrow happen. They do not confuse effort with results.

Chapter 24

Unions Love Bosses

Unions love Bosses because Bosses create a demand for their services. Bosses demonstrate to all concerned that employees need a union to protect them. Where bosses run rampant, unions will thrive and grow.

Management-union conflict is one of the major problems in the Canadian economy, and until it is modified by leadership on both sides, Canadians will continue to pay a heavy price in terms of unemployment, strikes and disruption of service. In large measure management is to blame for the sorry scheme of things in management union relations. Most companies that get a union deserve a union.

Management's and union's basic objectives are not incompatible. Most employees want good wages, interesting work, recognition, opportunity for advancement, reasonable job security, fair play, pride in their organization, good working conditions, and information on what is going on. Most companies want to make money, employ productive workers, have good employee and public relations, improve products and services, gain new markets, and make the best possible use of human and physical resources. It comes as a genuine surprise to management and union Bosses when this is pointed out to them. In many respects both sides want the same things. When these perceptions change on both sides — behavior starts to change.

Leaders in management and unions who are genuinely concerned with their employees and with their members will not have too many problems. Certainly there will be differences of opinion from time to time, but this is the way of the world when it is run by human beings.

Authority is given, but power is taken. Bosses are powerful because they have taken power away from employees: the power to think for themselves and make decisions on their own that affect the way they do their work. Unions are powerful because they have taken power from their members. Power is the curse of all Bosses, in management and unions alike, because it makes them into drivers, superiors of some kind, elitist, and agents of enforcement.

Leaders understand the dangers of taking power and using it for their own purpose. They know that power creates resentment and antagonism. Power does not create commitment to an organization, that is why powerful Bosses must always drive. Leaders enable employees to understand and share in the objectives and purpose of their company or organization by providing information on what is going on in abundance. The more input employees make into the decision-making process, the more committed to the end result they become. They have a stake in the outcomes, and they accept leadership to attain shared goals.

Paternalistic Bosses are surprised, indignant and outraged by employee "ingratitude", but paternalism is rapidly losing ground as a strategy to keep out the unions. Bosses are still hung up with the notion that the thing to do is buy loyalty and hard work. This notion is rooted in the way things were a long time ago when employees had no alternatives. Today there are alternatives: if you don't work you won't starve because society provides welfare and unemployment benefits. Employees are no longer ignorant and they are no longer afraid.

Bosses claim that the introduction of enlightened management methods is not acceptable to unions because the unions automatically resist anything suggested by management. Yet in some companies where union and management leaders have sat down and shared their perceptions of each other, remarkable progress has been made in developing new approaches to work problems.

Organized Labor never forgets that traditionally work improvement was introduced for one-sided gain and it is always suspicious of new ideas developed and initiated by management. Labor Bosses are often as reluctant as management Bosses to share power because it blurs their adversarial stand against each other. Conflict occurs when Bosses on both sides struggle for control over the work place like alien tribes battling for territorial rights. On each side Bosses try to strengthen their position at the other's expense and each in their way become managers of discontent. They constantly misinterpret the needs of employees because they are out of touch. On the union side this means getting out of step with the membership.

The ability or inability of Bosses to become leaders may well determine the eventual fate of unions. Wherever employees are given the opportunity to manage themselves, militant unions are less likely to appear.

Any new ideas for improved management-union relations will have to recognize that every organization has an obligation to help employees satisfy their needs, as well as the needs of customers and shareholders. In return employees must learn how to manage themselves in making a contribution to the goals of their organization. To achieve these ends, management will have to create a climate in which employees can freely participate in decision making at all levels.

These concepts will be interpreted by management Bosses as a threat to their managerial self-esteem, but if they are prepared to practise leadership they will find they can forestall many aspects of the adversarial system that presently encumbers them, and the whole economy. Many strikes occur by accident, when both sides are warily feeling each other out on how far they are prepared to go. As managers become more sophisticated in their understanding of human needs and how to satisfy them, the number of strikes will subside on the road from conflict to cooperation.

Chapter 25

Democracy in the Work Place

What is Worker-Power? It is a phrase used to describe Industrial Democracy. In practice it means that workers are given more control over the conditions in which they work and, in some cases, a share in the ownership. "Worker-Power is just another beautiful theory" according to a Boss I know who is a friend of mine. (As a friend, I like him very much. As a Boss, I can't stand his behavior.) Some beautiful theories can be murdered by a bunch of brutal facts, but glowing reports on various forms of Worker-Power suggest that this particular theory seems to be working out quite well.

In Sweden, Norway, West Germany, Spain, Yugoslavia, Peru, and other parts of the world, the theory and practice of Worker-Power is well under way. Is it the wave of the future? How did it come about in the first place, and what does it all add up to?

Amidst the crumbling cake of custom, we are losing the old religion based on the all-knowing, all-powerful leader. The tribal image of the "Old Man" is dying fast in the embers of history. Through the ages, blind respect for the "Old Man" has gradually been replaced by a series of dominant-submissive experiences in many situations. For example: Doctor-patient; Owner-renter; Policeman-citizen; Teacher-student; Lawyer-client; and Boss-servant.[1] What is going to take the place of these relationships as people become liberated with more knowledge and more power? The answer comes in the shape of power-equalization. The use of force is outmoded in organizations today. A quick glance at any of our social institutions shows quite clearly the inadequacy of using force to achieve the goals of human endeavor.

Out of sheer necessity, the Western World has given birth to a new era in the struggle of human beings to organise themselves for survival. Industrial democracy, Worker-Power, or whatever you want to call it, represents the attempts of many organizations to develop a new approach to the world-of-work. After centuries of trial and error in organizing the efforts of human beings through competitive relationships in pyramidal structures, enlightened leaders are now encouraging collaborative efforts with employees to manage the workplace.

On a global scale much the same thing is happening. As the world grows smaller the need for co-operation becomes greater. More and more countries find it to their advantage to get together and work out ways of harvesting natural resources. As organizations become more and more complex, they have to find ways of bringing people at all levels and getting them more involved in working out their problems. The Leaders are too far removed from the scene of the action to know what is best.

Over and above this, the birth of Worker-Power in

the West has been spurred by the growth of educational opportunities, television, and rising expectations. No longer are people content to work for Bosses in stifling superior-subordinate relationships. New awareness, new knowledge, and new life styles are all downplaying traditional values and the advantages of material gain. Most people still want to work, but they want more from their work. Much more. They want more control over the way they do their work, and more control over the place in which they do their work. Money is very important, but it is not enough to satisfy new needs aroused by new knowledge. Menial jobs go begging because in our society you are what you do. People want their work to be respected.

In the normal course of development, human beings grow up, gain new knowledge, break away from parental influence, and strike out on their own. In the family group the historic role of the father was to protect and provide until the young grew up. In the world of work the phrase "Old Man" is often applied to Bosses because they are unconsciously associated with the father figures known by all men since time immemorial. The paternalistic Boss perpetuates the role of the "Old Man" in a variety of ways. He tells them what to do; he punishes them when they do wrong; he rewards them when they do right. When one of his "children" offends him or challenges him, he drives him out.

For centuries this was the role of the "Old Man" because the vast majority of people were ignorant, illiterate, and uneducated. Long after they grew up and left home they were obliged to accept a submissive-dependent relationship with a variety of Bosses. In fact, their whole lives were lived in a series of superior-subordinate relationships. Today, in spite of the growing impact of education and television, most employees are still subjected to thinly veiled parent-child relationships with their Boss. It turns them off. Basically, Worker-Power is an expression of dissatisfaction with parent-child relationships in the world-of-work. Employees everywhere are "growing up" and they want to be treated as adults.

The Information Explosion of the 70's has made it very difficult for the "Old Man" to rule, particularly in the decision-making process which is becoming more complex and confusing than ever before.

Leaders know it is not *who* is right, but *what* is right that counts in making decisions. They listen to their employees' opinions. Bosses prefer to be right regardless of what is right. They prefer to listen to themselves.

Leaders recognize the primal current that flows deep beneath demands for self-control and self-management. They know that by integrating the needs of their people with the needs of the organization, they can harness the urge for growth, freedom, and achievement.

If we value democracy in Canada we must recognize that dictatorship in the workplace is counter-productive because political democracy depends on people who are capable of judging issues and electing leaders to govern them. You can't spend eight hours a day being dictated to and learn much about the democratic process. Unfortunately, most Bosses are the unwitting guardians of dictatorship. Bosses, like termites, are found in the woodwork of every organization busily nibbling away at the performance and productivity of their employees.

WORKER-POWER

The two basic objectives of Worker-Power are:
1) To develop new ways of resolving conflict and establishing co-operation.
2) To encourage higher productivity.

UNDER BOSSES:
Productivity just means Production.

UNDER LEADERS:
The emerging concept of productivity includes the satisfaction of needs through company operations plus the contributions of customers, employees, government, shareholders, and management.

Historically, unions came into being to protect workers from Bosses. Now, most unions have developed Bosses of their own who are equally as demanding and unyielding as their counter-parts in management. Like management, they tend to see Worker-Power as a threat to their hard-won rights and territorial claims. If Worker-Power takes over in a big way, who would need a union? Some experts in the field of industrial relations are openly saying that a smart capitalist should encourage Worker-Power as a way of keeping employees in line. Once people have a stake in the work place they would be less likely to disrupt it. Whatever the outcome in management-employee relations, there is little doubt that more and more organizations will have to find ways of introducing democratic measures into the workplace. If this doesn't happen the end result will be violence and disruption across the land, and we may wind up with a very undemocratic way of life indeed.

Bosses still have the opportunity to initiate various forms of worker-power through enlightened management systems, such as management by objectives, and job enrichment programmes. Properly introduced and properly applied, these new management systems provide the opportunity to teach and practise democratic principles in the workplace.

Most people are very well acquainted with Boss-Power because they have had to live with it in one way or another for most of their lives. Worker-Power is something new. Blue collar, white collar, and professional workers are taking the initiative away from Bosses in all kinds of organizations, in ways that would have been unthinkable just a few years ago. The failure of union, business, and government Bosses to get together and agree on ways of meeting this new challenge will bring crisis and challenge into the lives of every person in Canada.

The answer to Worker-Power is enlightened leadership in management and unions alike, and there are signs of awakening interest in a number of organizations. A few companies have been practising modified forms of Worker-Power through profit-sharing plans of various kinds. Shelley Lush, the President of Supreme Aluminum Company in Toronto, wants every employee to have a piece of the action in his company. In a speech to the Winnipeg Chamber of Commerce in 1975 he had this to say:

> Let's go to our employees, the people with whom we work, who should be our allies and our partners, but with whom instead we find ourselves fighting and fighting across Canada like we have never fought before, and with whom battles are increasing daily and with whom co-operation is diminishing. Let's go to our employees and offer them a deal, give to them a piece of the action, and ask them to join us as a partner, so that together we can start to tap the almost untouched potential that exists among our human

assets. Let's start to give our human assets the same kind of attention we have given to our fixed assets over the past 100 years.

I have had the privilege of working with the managers of the Supreme Aluminum Company and I can assure you that every one is a Leader.

Another outstanding leader is Dean Muncaster, President of Canadian Tire Corporation. This is what he has to say about managing people.

> Attracting and retaining competent and highly motivated people is the major problem facing most businesses today. One way to accomplish this objective is to provide employees with a profit-sharing plan with share ownership benefits, which will give them a sense of belonging. This is the path that Canadian Tire Corporation has been following and much of our company's success can be attributed to the profit-sharing plan which led to greater employee participation in company affairs, and more direct delegation of responsibility.

In the five year period from 1970 to 1975 Canadian Tire earnings have grown from $212,000,000 to $561,000,000. A 20-year employee is worth about $396,000 in stock and shares. A first-line supervisor at Canadian Tire is expected to make decisions without getting approval from anyone. He is expected to manage himself, and he does. "We believe very strongly in the true delegation of authority and responsibility," says Muncaster. "If you have hired a guy to do a job, let him do it. As long as you are confident that you have the right person, it is our view that you will end up with far better performance."

Why do Bosses leave the initiative to unions? Leaders don't. They get the unions involved and make sure they understand what is going on before some new method is introduced. Union members should be invited to take part in management seminars with staff from all levels if their co-operation is required to implement new work procedures. This is a very effective way of creating mutual understanding and respect.

The absence of leadership can lead to a dramatic form of Worker-Power. In 1974 in Central Wales the General Transport & Workers Union set up special union "courts" to put misbehaving Bosses on trial. Bosses who get in late for work, slip up on their jobs, or stay out too long for lunch, are to be brought before the workers for judgment. The workers said they planned to give Bosses a taste of their own medicine. The evidence against accused bosses is to be heard by a jury of workers. Anyone found guilty of a minor offence will be warned to "watch it" in the future. More serious offences will be punished by requesting the company to cut the salary of the offending Boss. If any company refuses to act on the court's verdict, the workers will stage an all-out strike.

The union court plans to keep a close watch on Bosses in factories, garages, and shops throughout the area and will keep dossiers on their good and bad points.

Bosses take notice, this could happen to you.

Many Bosses think that management science is a substitute for leadership. The plus factor in management is leadership. Leadership is the extra skill that makes the difference between success and mediocrity — in management and unions alike. Leadership creates the desire in people to want to do more and to be more. Leadership must create hope, desire, vision, and excitement. Leaders get out there and see what is going on.

They can bring work groups together and generate enthusiasm in a way which no Boss can. Dynamic, enlightened Leaders make things happen, they inspire and enthuse people. They shape the future; they make tomorrow happen. Leaders know that management is not the direction of things, it is the development of people.

Leaders know that every employee, regardless of his or her schooling, is a potential inventor, a pioneer, a voyageur into the yet-unfathomed depths of Inner as well as the Outer Space.

The role of the effective leader in any organization is an educational one. Educating people to manage themselves is the most effective way to harness the human energy potential of Worker-Power.

1. *I am indebted to Dr. B. Landuyl, formerly of Detroit University for this example.*

Chapter 26

Where It's At
And What To Do

There seems to be little doubt that the public in general is losing faith in the way its institutions are being managed. Big Business, Big Government, and Big Unions tend to lose touch with their members. More and more employees in large organizations complain that they feel cut off and not involved. A recent survey of the Metro Toronto Police Force reveals a major reason why morale is low: policemen feel their superiors are out of touch with them; are too autocratic; too much like Bosses instead of Leaders. Traditional management, coupled with a better educated work-force and rising expectations commonly add up to a potentially explosive situation in any organization. This is one reason why "small" is becoming "Beautiful." Individuals and groups are tending to break away from larger units to go their own way. More people are dropping out to escape from being stifled and reduced to a cipher, a digit, or a file card. The storm over Quebec's declared intent to separate from the rest of Canada is an example – on a larger scale – of the increasing desire of groups to seek their own identity and manage themselves. Of all the provinces Quebec has been made to feel the most subordinate and inferior over the years and it has bitterly resented its unequal status. The present demands for independence may be an over-reaction to the long years of subordination in a parent-child relationship with Ottawa. The diagram on page 138 may help to portray the shift from superior-subordinate relationships on an unequal basis to leader-team relationships based on democratic co-equal status.

Bosses unconsciously perpetuate the patriarchal system which has dominated the world for centuries. The historic role of the father figure has been to protect and provide for offspring, and then drive them away to fend for themselves. Deep down, Bosses see employees as members of an extended family, and when they don't perform too well they want to drive them out. It's an instinctive reaction; they want to get rid of them, but very often they can't. They have to live with them. This creates problems. A Boss does not know how to handle this situation so he takes it out on his employees. Even if a Boss is generous at times, employees still wind up frustrated because they resent their dependency on "The Old Man". It is at odds with their instinctive desire to manage themselves. Deep down, they don't really want to work for someone else. They would rather manage themselves in a meaningful way, using their own initiative and enterprise.

Leaders understand the psychological bondage that employees feel and how it can reduce performance and productivity. Leaders go out of their way to create opportunities for growth, learning, and

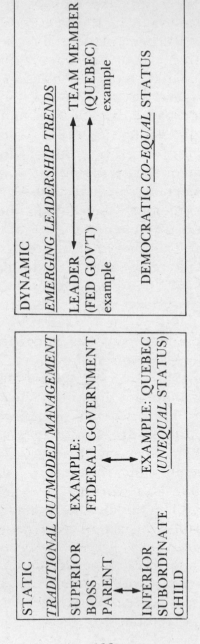

STATIC

TRADITIONAL OUTMODED MANAGEMENT

SUPERIOR   EXAMPLE:
BOSS   FEDERAL GOVERNMENT
PARENT

                EXAMPLE: QUEBEC
                (*UNEQUAL STATUS*)
INFERIOR
SUBORDINATE
CHILD

DYNAMIC

EMERGING LEADERSHIP TRENDS

LEADER   TEAM MEMBER
(FED GOV'T)   (QUEBEC)
example   example

DEMOCRATIC *CO-EQUAL STATUS*

freedom on the job. Aside from productivity they know that "the absence of opportunities for self-expression, recognition and fulfillment which come from a meaningful and significant role in the organization instills feelings of inferiority which color the employees relations with the larger society and diminish his general life satisfaction."[1]

As the world grows smaller, and organizations grow bigger, it is vital to National Security – in the broadest sense of the term – to learn how to *WORK TOGETHER*. If we fail to do this at national, provincial, local and company levels, Canada will eventually fragment into a thousand bits and pieces and become easy prey for "Hungry Gobblers" around the world. Bosses exist at all levels of our society and they feed on memories of the past. In the words of Marshall McLuhan, they are "stumbling into the future backwards." Such behaviour is a luxury we cannot afford in an Age when Man, for the first time in history, is capable of consciously planning to make the future happen through enlightened leadership and effective management.

The decline and fall of Bosses is occurring from practical necessity rather than idealistic concern. Many organizations today, will freely admit that they are having trouble with their human resources. They are desperate for ways to deal with people problems. Not all Bosses can be easily converted into leaders, although in some cases it can happen very quickly, and very dramatically – when they finally "see the light". When a Boss learns, understands, and accepts, that Leaders really do get better results, he starts to change his behaviour; he starts acting like a Leader. It just doesn't make sense to keep on "BOSSING."

There is a natural resistance to change in all of us because of the effort involved in unlearning what we already know. Very often we resist the way the need for change is communicated. Bosses are not stupid. Far from it. Often they are very intelligent people who have developed a high level of expertise in dealing with things. They were promoted because of their ability to deal with Things, rather than People! They become Bosses because in most cases they have never had the opportunity to learn anything about leadership in modern management. In many companies today, Bosses at all levels are being told, in effect, "become a Leader, or step down." Early retirement or a non-supervisory position is often the choice presented to them. The facts show that companies that spend the most attention to developing Leaders are the companies that wind up leading the field.

So, what does it all add up to? If you are a Boss, the first step is to admit it to yourself. Think about the historic evolution of the Boss and what the word "Boss" symbolizes to the people who are being bossed. If you really understand why people react to Bosses in one way, and to Leaders in another, you will start to change your own behaviour. Nobody can *force* you to change your ideas, anymore than you can *force* your employees to be more productive. When you have reached the stage of understanding you can look around and start to identify some of the important needs of your employees that you may have overlooked along the way.

Your most important job is to train and develop your employees so that they can manage themselves with a minimum of supervision. Freedom on the job is an important key. Under the right conditions most people will respond to the challenge of growth, which is the challenge of Life itself. You *can* learn how to keep your people ALIVE on the job, and doing this will not only bring you greater performance and productivity, it will make you stretch and grow as a person. You can't help people to improve without improving yourself. A true Leader in the world of work provides his people with the rich experience of being able to satisfy some of their deep psychological needs. When you start helping your employees to meet *their* needs, you will find that they will be much more likely to help you meet some of *your* needs. It can be done, and it is being done. *YOU CAN DO IT TOO!* A wise leader once said that a thousand mile journey starts with the first step. *Make that first step NOW.*

1. *Nightingdale, Donald. "Industrial Democracy", Business Quarterly, Fall 1976.*

BIBLIOGRAPHY

Barrett, F. D. "Everyman's Guide to Time Management". *Business Quarterly,* Spring 1973.

Berne, Eric. *Games People Play.* Ballantine 1964.

Boettenger, H. "Is Management Really an Art?" *Harvard Business Review,* Jan/Feb 1975.

Bull, Warren. "Compensation Managers — Let's Not Sleepwalk the '70's". *Business Quarterly,* Winter 1973.

Conference Board Anthology. *Challenge to Leadership.* Free Press 1973.

Cooper, J. D. *How to Get More Done in Less Time.* Doubleday, 1971.

de Bono, Edward. *Lateral Thinking for Management* AMA New York.

Dickson, Paul. *The Future of the Workplace.* Weybright and Talley, 1975.

Donnelly, John F. "Participative Management at Work" *Harvard Business Review* Jan/Feb 1977.

Drucker, Peter. *The Practice of Management.* McGraw Hill 1954.
The Effective Executive. Pan 1970.
The Age of Discontinuity. Harper Row 1968.

Forrester, J. W. *Industrial Dynamics.* MIT Press 1961.

Foy, Nancy and Herman Godon. "Worker participation contrasts in three countries" *Harvard Business Review,* May/June 1976.

Gellerman, Saul. *Management by Motivation.* AMA 1963.

Hayakawa, S. I. *Language in Thought and Action.* Harcourt-Bruce 1956.

Herzberg, F. *Work and the Nature of Man.* World Publishing 1966.

Jay, Antony. *Corporation Man.* Pocket Books 1973.
Management & Machiavelli. Pelican.

Johnson, R. T. and W. Ouchi. "Made in America Under Japanese Management". *Harvard Business Review* Sept/Oct 1974.

Johnson, Wendell. *Your Most Enchanted Listener.* Harper.

Lee, Irving J. *Language Habits in Human Affairs.* Harper 1956.

Likert, Rensis. *The Human Organization.* McGraw Hill 1967.

Loen, Raymond O. *Managing More by Doing Less.* McGraw Hill 1971.

Maslow, A. *Motivation and Personality.* Harper Row 1970.

McGregor, Douglas. *The Human Side of Enterprise.* McGraw Hill 1960.

Mehrabian, A. *Silent Messages.* Wadsworth 1971.

Mills, Ted. "Human Resources — Why the New Concern?" *Harvard Business Review* March/April 1975.

Mintzberg, H. "The Manager's Job, Folklore and Fact" *Harvard Business Review* July/August 1975.

Myers, M. Scott. *Every Employee a Manager.* McGraw Hill 1970.

Nightingdale, Donald. "Industrial Democracy: A Strategy for Improving Productivity and Labor-Management Relations". *Business Quarterly,* Fall 1976.

Parker-Kleemier-Parker. *Front Line Leadership.* McGraw Hill 1969.

Report of the Task Force to the Secretary of HEW. *Work in America.* USA 1973.

Tarrant, John J. *Drucker.* Cahners Books 1976.

Webber, Ross A. *Time and Management.* Van Nostrand 1972.

Whiteside, Lyn W. *Effective Management Techniques for Getting Things Done.* Parker 1968.